Tips From The Trenches

for scrummasters & agile coaches

YvesHanoulle

Tips From The agile Trenches

for scrummasters & agile coaches

YvesHanoulle

ISBN 9789464209716

Leanpub

Tweet This Book!

Please help YvesHanoulle by spreading the word about this book on Twitter!

The suggested hashtag for this book is #TipsFromTheTrenches.

Find out what other people are saying about the book by clicking on this link to search for this hashtag on Twitter:

#TipsFromTheTrenches

Also By YvesHanoulle

Who is agile? Volume 1

Arduino met Geike

Who is agile in Nigeria?

The Leadership Game

Arduino with Geike

CoachRetreat

Who is agile in South Africa?

Our house in the garden

Who is agile in Australia & New Zealand?

Programmeren voor kinderen

Create your own manifesto

PO as a service workshop

Who is agile in Ukraine?

Who is agile in India

Das Leadership-Spiel

The Scaling Ball Game

Pair Programming

Community TIPS for hiring great people

Who is agile in Singapore?

Gereedschapskist voor de Agile Coach – Visualisatievoorbeelden

I dedicate this book to all the teams everyone who contributed to this book worked with. These people suffered from the mistakes we made, that we now call experience.

Contents

1. Foreword

This books is filled with great tips, but do not fall fool to the idea that some one of these tips will make a quantum jump in your productivity or quality.

That kind of professional improvement generally comes in small steps over a fairly long period of time, so be patient with these tips. Try one (not all at once), and notice what difference if makes, if any. Pay attention to the Satir Change Model[1], and be prepared for a tip to actually tip you backward for a while. Be prepared to stick with it, to practice and gain experience. Then, when you reach a plateau, that's the time to pick another tip.

Jerry Weinberg

Receiving this text, was the last interaction I had with Jerry a few weeks before he died.
Jerry uses every interaction I had with him or others to coach. I have read many of his books, and I think I advised all the ones I read to friends, clients, family members. I'm glad I was able to follow PSL and AYE. I'm sad the world has lost such a great person. I'm proud he agreed to use this tip as a foreword.

Y

---

[1]https://stevenmsmith.com/ar-satir-change-model/

2. Preface

Improvement

The quote I tweeted, was send to me by Stacia in a private mail conversation. For me, it explains a lot how I go through life. yes, some feedback hurts, and it will happen that I get emotional, yet most of the time, for me I treat all kind of feedback as data.

Ever since I was a kid, I looked at the world, with eyes, trying to make things better. More than once I had friends and lovers telling me, why can't you just be happy. What these people failed to see, was that I was happy. For me, being happy does not mean accepting the world as it is.
Competitive people want to improve themselves. I mostly want to improve the world around me. (And yes that includes setting an example myself)

When I talk to friends, in the agile community, I regularly

think, wow, this is a great idea, I should try that.

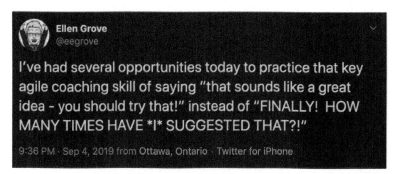

I've had several opportunities today to practice that key agile coaching skill of saying "that sounds like a great idea - you should try that!" instead of "FINALLY! HOW MANY TIMES HAVE *I* SUGGESTED THAT?!"

9:36 PM · Sep 4, 2019 from Ottawa, Ontario · Twitter for iPhone

Great idea

When I hear great idea's I want to share them with the world. I use the ideas, I retell the stories and I tweet about them. As much as I like twitter, as a content store, it's weak.

Hence this book is born, a place where agile minded people can share their tips from the trenches. I'm extremely grateful that so many people wanted to share a tip. Some of these are controversial, although I don't agree with ever tip, I find it important to give a broad look at options, not just options Yves likes. That said, I'm really blown away about most tips.

I get e-mails from people, asking me, what do you think of this draft? And after I read the tip, I want to add it asap to the book. What a community! Humans are so smart.
I'm so happy this community allows me to share that wisdom.

You will see some big agile names in the book. You know them, you know they are smart, and yes you will love their tips. After you devoured their tips, have a look at all the people you don't know. Some might be famous in their country, in their company, some might be working happy in a corner, improving the world, without most of us knowing them. Yet all of them have great tips. Enjoy them.

If you want to know the story behind the tips, together with Vasco Duarte I am creating an audio addition to the book[1].

Yves Hanoulle

[1]https://oikosofyseries.com/tips_from_the_trenches_the_audio_project

3. We are uncovering better ways of developing software

3.1 We are continuously uncovering

In 1983 I bought my first computer. A Commodore 64. Soon, I wrote my first code. In BASIC. That was thirty-seven years ago. From there, it didn't take long before I earned money from writing code. That was at the age of nineteen, during the first year of my computer science studies.

However, it wasn't until recently, during a conversation with my girlfriend Kim, who is just taking up programming, that I realized that when I wrote my first code, the field of software development had only existed for about forty years. It is a young field.

I learned how to code without automatically refactoring development tools, without being able to run code in the cloud, without unit testing, without automated pipelines, without continuous integration, and even without StackOverflow. We didn't even have the internet. All of this simply didn't exist thirty years ago.

The field of software development has evolved rigorously during its short existence. We went from the very first computers to a ubiquitous worldwide presence of software on a magnitude of devices in about seventy years.

And we have learned so much.

If you consider the methodologies and approaches for software development over the years a similar pattern emerges. Back in 1983, I didn't know much about methodologies. Yes, waterfall existed, but my projects weren't large enough to apply it. It wasn't until my first job at a consultancy, in 1994, that I first encountered waterfall projects. It wasn't pretty. They went over budget, over time, and under-delivered. Project managers ruled relentlessly, processes were strict, and developers were mere resources.

But we learned. We started to realize that requirements change and feedback was useful, so we'd better take it into account. A new generation of methodologies emerged, such as the Unified Process and the Spiral Model, introducing increments and iterations, albeit usually in cycles of several months.

In the mid-1990s, I got acquainted with the Dynamic Systems Development Method (DSDM). DSDM has increments and iterations at heart and it introduced much shorter cycles. Along with improvements in languages, tools, and frameworks, we now delivered increments in iterations of six or eight weeks. And for the first time, these iterations included all activities necessary to deliver, such as design, coding, testing, integration, and releasing increments to the customer.

We learned again. The shorter the feedback loops, the higher the quality. And, the more rituals and ceremonies we could make redundant, the better and faster we became. Bye-bye big-upfront designs. Bye-bye Gantt charts. So long rigor project plans.

As a result, in 1998, my team and I developed the Smart approach that combined these learnings with again improved tooling, including code generation. It allowed us to shorten our iterations again, to lengths of three to four weeks. Not too long after that, my team and I learned about extreme programming (XP), and with it, we discovered the merits of refactoring, continuous integration, unit testing, and even autonomy, which shortened our iterations again.

Then in 2001, the Agile Manifesto was published.

It is needless to say, almost twenty later, that the Agile Manifesto made an unimaginably big impact on the world. It is a major driver in changing organizations in many different industries. For us, the Manifesto was a strong confirmation that we were on the right track. Smart was an agile approach, and it's popularity piggybacked on the evangelization of agile.

Then, we bumped into Scrum, which soon became more popular than all of the other agile approaches together. Scrum almost became synonymous with agile. Due to its simplicity Scrum attracted people from many other fields to software development. At the same time, our tooling improved again. Git largely improved version control systems. JUnit made unit testing tangible. Refactoring finally got supported out-of-the-box. Clear many impediments from our paths, we again were able to move faster. Our iterations shortened again, to one to two weeks.

Moreover, we learned that the process of making rituals and ceremonies redundant to become better and faster never stops. It is continuous.

The ideas, values, and principles of the Agile Manifesto remain extremely valuable. But Scrum is not the end game. Moving forward continuously means that its rituals and ceremonies will become redundant as soon as we can move beyond them. Exactly following the most important part of the Agile Manifesto.

We are uncovering better ways of developing software by doing it and helping others do it.

Where does that leave us today? To cut a decade short. We now reap the benefits of continuous delivery, and being able to automatically test and deploy our code in the cloud. We leverage microservices architectures, DevOps, and infrastructure-as-code, allowing teams to prune even more overhead from their approaches.

For the last seven to eight years, I've helped organizations to move along these lines. Every time, the results were similar. Despite the resistance from traditional agile and Scrum representatives, we made more and more of the rituals and ceremonies redundant that we so happily introduced twenty years ago.

We now deliver individual features. Continuously. Therefore, there's no need to plan and fit our work items into iterations or sprints. We stopped doing sprints, but rather deliver features multiple times per day. Without having to fit work into sprints, there was no need anymore for low-level estimates. We dropped those too. And instead of organizing day-long refinement workshops at the start of sprints, we rather briefly discuss each work item on the day we pick it up.

Each of our work items only requires a small subset of the skills of the whole team. Therefore, each work item is picked up exactly when we need to deliver it, but also exactly by who can deliver it. Tiny teams of one to three people work on tiny work items, for maybe one or two days, deliver it, and then disband again, to reform new tiny teams, often in different compositions. I refer to these teams as microteams, as a reference to microservices.

Again we learned to deliver software better and faster. We made the rituals and ceremonies of the current generation of agile approaches redundant, without losing the good parts. So bye-bye sprint planning and refinements. Bye-bye story point estimation. So long sprints.

Still, we completely adhere to the Agile Manifesto, which clearly states that our highest priority is to satisfy the customer through early and continuous delivery of valuable software. Today we just deliver even smaller features, in even shorter cycles, with even smaller teams, in smaller components.

As an example, my current team builds a microservices platform for an IoT company. We bring the platform one step further every day. We don't have sprints. We don't estimate our work items. Our testing and pipelines are fully automated, and our infrastructure is immutable. We have very few ceremonies left and simply answer one question every day: what small problem are we solving today? We operate in microteams of constantly varying compositions and deliver work items multiple times per day. And actually, it's a breeze.

If there's one thing I've learned from twenty years of agile and thirty-five years in this industry is that all methodologies are temporary, including agile approaches. We are continuously uncovering better ways of working.

I'm already curious about how we will fare in the next decade.

Sander Hoogendoorn

3.2 You will never arrive at THE destination

The saddest and the gladdest part of Agile is that you will never arrive at THE destination. At the very heart of agile is the culture of kaizen a.k.a. continuous improvement. You are NOT agile if you are NOT constantly changing your thinking and hence your process. Even before the agile manifesto was written in 2001, many of us have been constantly trying new experiments and trying to uncover even better ways of working. And yes there is a long way to go.

As ScrumMaster or Coach or Change Agent or Leader on teams, if you can successfully instill the kaizen culture, I think we have set in the right direction (at least from agile's perspective.) Often teams implement a set of agile practices and they just focus on doing them well. This misses the point of agile. We need to constantly audit if these practices are still helping. What happens if we discard a specific practice? Now that the team is at a specific stage on their journey, can we tweak the practice to have a larger impact? This thought process is extremely curial for a continuous improvement culture.

For example: When we start our agile journey, having a clear visibility into who is doing what and getting the team to collaborate is a challenge. A daily scrum meeting is a good way to address these challenges. After doing the daily scrum for a few months, its time to challenge its purpose. If you still need the daily scrum because we don't have the visibility or because the team is not helping each other and collaborating, then we need to change something. If we've addressed those challenges, then again, we need to identify what our other challenges and how we can look for other practices or at the very least tweak our daily scrum to address them. I typically use a value-stream map to help me with such exercises.

In my experience, to be successful at Continuous Improvement you need 3 important ingredients:
Safe Fail Experimentation - When you try new ideas, not all ideas will work as expected. The new idea might make the situation worse. Are you trying this experiment in a small controlled environment where its safe to fail? Are you trying 2 or 3 such small ideas in parallel to really A/B test the ideas?
Inspect and Adapt - When we try an experiment can we say with confidence that things have improved or gone bad? To have this kind of confidence, you need a bit of scientific way of measurement. You need a way to quantify the current situation/state, a hypothesis of what would change and a clear way to measure them as you try your experiment. Without this mindset, you might just be trying a bunch of things and letting you bias decide to pursue or quit. This is not a continuous improvement culture.
Internalise the Insights: Lastly, every experiment will teach you something. Are you ready to accept the results with a neutral standpoint? If you can do that, then you can gain real insights from such experiments and internalize them.

Naresh Jain

3.3 Become a continuous learner and model that...

Assume you will need support beyond the information you received in your scrummaster certification training. Become a continuous learner and model that for your team(s). Find your internal SM forum, a local Agile user group, and/or other group you can feel safe in for asking and answering questions on a frequent basis. Look for a place you can both learn and contribute. Also attend local and/or regional conferences related to your work as a scrummaster, then share what you learn with your colleague.

Diana Larsen

3.4 Create a high-bandwidth work environment

I've never heard a team (co-located or remote) say "our communication is perfect." Which means we can start with the premise that communication on any team is going to be a challenge. On a distributed team, we need to go even further to make it easy to stay in touch. It shouldn't be technically challenging, the equipment shouldn't get in the way, and we shouldn't always have to schedule a meeting to talk to someone.

A simple recipe for making remote communication easy is:

- Have great Internet
- Minimize background noise
- Use excellent equipment
- Embrace video
- Work out loud

Being in the same room with others is powerful because of all the sensory input that we have. We can see when someone is tired. We can sense when someone is frustrated. We can show our appreciation by giving high fives or celebrating together. All of these things create a collaborative environment.

When we go remote, we lose a lot of that physical and visual input. Being a team through our screens is different than doing it face to face, but that doesn't mean it has to be worse.

Lisette Sutherland

3.5 Becoming Better through the Community

My tip is to look beyond your team and organisation to grow as an agile practitioner and become involved in the greater community.

My agile journey deepened when I discovered the Dallas-Fort Worth Scrum user group. At the time, I was a project manager trying to introduce an agile approach in a digital agency setting. My goal was to learn from experienced practitioners and thought leaders; I was more interested in the content than the networking opportunities. The group had a simple mission: to help one another do better today than they did yesterday.

I learned about topics and heard from speakers that I might not have been exposed to otherwise. People shared their challenges and successes so that we could all learn from them. When I left a meetup, I had new ideas to try or to share in my workplace. I found a mentor with whom to seek advice and share successes. The teams I worked with improved as a result of my involvement in the DFW agile community.

A few years later, I went from shy attendee to group organizer. I found people were happy to be invited to speak to the group and generous in sharing their wisdom and experience. Our local user group grew significantly, and relationships deepened in the community. We heard more about the increasing agility of local companies through our interactions and supported one another through job and company transitions. I became a better agilist as I practiced what I'd learned from the community in different work environments.

The DFW Scrum user group I grew up with represents the ideal for internal communities of practice I've helped start. The friendships forged through the community serve as a model for the coaching and mentoring relationships I enjoy now. Today's local user groups provide opportunities for those I coach to connect with others and learn more. As a conference speaker myself, I choose co-presenters and topics that will expand my range and further my practice of agile. Sharing my knowledge and experiences, whether one-on-one or in a setting of 100-plus, enables me to discover new insights while encouraging others to do better today than they did yesterday.

I invite you to participate in the agile community at large, and I hope we learn from one another some day soon.

Allison Pollard

3.6 Turn Up the Good

I suspect that the most important aspect of Scrum is the concept of "inspect and adapt".

Regardless of what we know at the beginning of today we will learn something new during the day. If that is true, then applying what we have learned today in our work tomorrow could lead to massive improvements over time.

It's like the compounding effect in a savings account. If the interest is compounded daily we will earn a lot more over time than if it is compounded monthly, and a great deal more than if it is compounded yearly.

If we can reflect, tune, and adjust day after day those little increases multiply and while the improvement of any one day is small, the result over time is great.

I learned this a long time ago: If we do a very short retrospective at the end of each day we have an opportunity to take advantage of the impact of compounding.

To make it even better, I've found that if we look for something that went well today and find a way to amplify it the very next day the result is surprising. That is, rather than look for things that need fixing, focus on whatever went well. It's energizing to build on our successes.

I call this "Turn Up the Good". You might want to try it and see if it works for you.

Woody Zuill

3.7 Study the manifesto

Ever since I read the manifesto, it has been my guide.
When I'm stuck at work, with a team, a person or anything at some point I go back to the manifesto and I read it and reread it, until it triggers a solution in me.
And I mean I read both pages.

And read every sentence and every word of every sentence. When I did, I came to realise that many people hardly know about that first sentence.

We are uncovering better ways of developing software by doing it and helping others do it.

Many people focus on the next 4 statements, yet there is so much info in that first sentence.

- Let's start with the obvious: yes the manifesto was written for people who write software. I do think that it's ideas can be ported to outside IT, yet people that do this, should translate the manifesto to their economy.

F ex What does "working software" mean in context of HR?

- uncovering & helping are written in the current tense.

It's about doing and doing it now. For me, this is also about life long learning. When I'm asked to help a team, I want to discover with them what is the better way. What was the better way for the last team I helped, might not be the better way for the next team.

- by doing it and helping others

This sentence is why I have personally chosen not to become a full time trainer. I want to stay with my feet in the mud, together with teams.

- We

For me, this word means the agile community. yes I know when it was written it meant 17 white men. I don't care. When I say study the manifesto, I don't mean study it so that you know what these 17 men are trying to tell you. For that I would advise you to work with one of the 16 remaining authors. Instead when I say study the manifesto, I mean, study it to understand what it means to you.

These are 4 examples about what studying the manifesto tells me.
I would love to read what you learn(ed) from the manifesto.

Yves Hanoulle

3.8 Visualize More !

Nothing enables collaboration and a shared understanding of the work, flow of work, agreements as a good visualization. Use a whiteboard and the wide variety of Post-its that is available. Or tape flipcharts to your walls if you don't have any available whiteboards at your office.

Visualize more

Visualize your vision. Your roadmap. Capture and visualize your working agreement so that you can hold each other accountable to it and regularly review if you honor it or not. Visualize your work and your workflow. If you keep track of your work in jira, visualize the flow and what is required for a ticket to move between stages in the flow. The discussion about the flow itself will invite you to discover if you actually have the same understanding of it, or if you regard the rules of the game differently. Visualize where work comes from. And where work goes. Map your stakeholders, their needs and goals. Visually keep track of how well you are adopting new habits. Visualize your dependencies and blockers so that you can act on them. Create posters for your achievements and proud moments.

A good visualization also makes work more fun, invites to communication and encourages engagement.

Just do it. Visualize more!

Jimmy Janlén

3.9 Holding Space for growth

When I became a Scrum Master, I asked my coach what he does when he joins a new team. He said that he fills all gaps. That made a lot of sense to me. Taking care of the things not being done must certainly help the Scrum team and the organisation. But at some point I started to wonder: How will the team ever become self-organized if there is nothing left to pick up and do?

So now whenever I join a new team as Scrum Master I watch. And I may pick up some of the things that are not taken care of. I introduce structure where it's missing. But never in all places. And I always make sure some things are not being taken care of by me. So that tasks and responsibilities can be picked up by those who want to take the challenge. And there is something else I'm doing which I think is an important ingredient to make that approach work: I trust them to be able to do it.

During my coaching education we were asked what we see in our peer-learners. It was easy to name traits I saw in others. But I felt terrible hearing all the things that others saw in me. They made me so much bigger than I thought I was. And I kept wondering how they could possibly see those things in me. Over time I noticed a few of those things come true. And for others ... I could sometimes be like that but never consciously. Until I heard somebody else say the same about me. And I asked what they were seeing or hearing me do that made them assign me this trait. And now that I had a cue I could start working on the last remaining bit. The one that I was named after in the training and that was the last for me to fully discover and become.

Knowing what others see in you can be very powerful. And even if you don't accept those things immediately, they will eventually work their ways and shine through.
I was always the one to see the good in others, even as a child. You can call that naïve but I believe it helped others to become more of that good thing because I was giving it room. People will develop the behaviour that you see in them. I was lucky to have been teachers' darling. I could hardly do anything wrong. I was excused for missing homework, … And I saw plenty of those that were labelled as the lazy ones, the ones who just didn't get things. And that's what they became (at least as long as they stayed with the same teachers).

Nowadays I make a point of telling people and teams what I see in them and help them acquire the knowledge and skills they need on that path. And I try to stay flexible enough so that they can become even bigger or different to that.
I create and hold the space that allows others to grow. I let them know about these things so that they can make conscious choices about it. And I leave the room for them for however long they need.

If you asked me about my advice to thriving people and teams: Be curious, try to become aware of the potential that's available around you. Be intentional about developing this potential by letting others know what you see and pay attention to their speed so that they always have enough room to grow but not so much so that they stumble.

Irene Kuhn

3.10 Don't forget to mine for conflict

Scrum Teams bloom when there is high team morale, positive energy, good mood, and when people genuinely like each other. It's a beautiful sight to see.

And it might seem that this is the ultimate goal of the Scrum Master is to create this perfect environment within and around the team. Or is it?

Obviously, having great team dynamics is good because it encourages collaboration and makes self-organization much easier.

However, beware of the trap of "continuous celebration" - when you are so happy about what you achieved, that you no longer improve.

I once worked with a team for a short time when I was still quite new to the role. They were the best! The most positive and enthusiastic team of all. Always happy, always smiling. And it wasn't just fun and games - they were also delivering done Increments of the product.

In retrospectives, we usually had nothing to discuss though. We would get a couple of notes, mostly about how great things are going, and no ideas of what can be improved. Sometimes, not a single thing that went wrong.

Wow, we were on top of the world.

I then moved from the team, but I know that nothing changed for them for the longest time - they still had nothing to improve.

And while it seemed like a good thing, in the long term the team disappeared. As it turned out, one of the team members was not too happy about the work they were doing. They were stuck doing the boring testing part, but they wanted to do more. Somehow it never came up during the retrospective. Or maybe it wasn't brought strongly enough for the team to be willing to make a change. Eventually, that person found a new role outside of the team and moved away.

For me, it is a sad story. Don't get me wrong - it is totally ok for teams to change and for team members to find new growth opportunities. But not because of unresolved issues that were not addressed in a long time.

It was a huge missed opportunity to improve, and the Scrum framework provided the team with all the means of inspecting and adapting and they didn't use them. That's the saddest part.

As Patrick Lencioni said in his book "Five Dysfunctions of a Team", a leader's job is to mine for conflict sometimes. Same goes for Scrum Masters - your job is to mine for improvement.. at all times.

If you find yourself in a similar situation where everything is perfect, don't hesitate to steer the pot a little - a short uncomfortable moment might as well save your Scrum team.

DariaBagina

3.11 Asynchronous management: Simplicity in a digital workplace

In a digital workplace, communication can be done in two different ways: synchronous (in real-time) and asynchronous (just-in-time). As the agile community continues to debate the need for more synchronous, face-to-face and high band-width methods of communication through agile ceremonies, the world is moving in the opposite direction making re-mote work and by extension asynchronous communication inevitable. High performing remote agile teams usually com-municate asynchronously by default. Team members in such teams do not depend on being present (online) at the same time for the sole purpose of exchanging information effec-tively. Instead they co-create a digital workplace and foster a culture in which effectiveness in communication is independ-ent of the time at which information is spread or consumed. Like any other major shift in mindset and behavior, it takes time to replace the old agile habits of face-to-face meetings or video calls with asynchronous communication methods such as long-form texts, pre-recorded videos, well-structured task management systems, deliberately placed comments, etc.

To accelerate this transition, you should follow the following tips:

1. minimize the number of communication tools you use.
2. stop having mandatory meetings (including daily scrums, retrospective meetings, etc)

Combining these two tips can guide any remote agile team to create more transparency over information making it possible for each individual to access any information they need, exactly when they need it, hence resulting in more effective communication without the need to exchange information in meetings. This approach also has a side effect: every meeting becomes purposeful and engaging as meetings become the last resort for communicating, not the first choice. Asynchronous management of work, empowers individuals to interact effectively by leveraging simple processes and modern tools.

Molood Ceccarelli

4. by doing it

4.1 Observe

Observe.

Henrik Kniberg

4.2 Question your teams intimacy

Collaboration is not just about working together or tolerating each other. Real collaboration happens when teams redefine their intimacy with each other. We all understand collaboration when it comes to friends and family. However at workplaces we struggle to build relationships based on trust and respect. It's almost understood that work people cannot share an intimate bond. As a scrum master the way to go about this is to create an environment of mutual trust and respect. This will not be an overnight job, however small steps towards this journey is important. From healthy confrontation to vocal admiration everything makes a difference. In this process you might lose people, gain respect and maybe at times understand your own self better.

This level of intimacy is threatening and scary. We are not used to such environments outside our close circle. Human mind will automatically warn you against the circumstances. It's important to hold the fort and do the right thing. One cannot build this level intimacy unless we are willing to let go of the shackles that hold us back. Awareness about your actions and most importantly our reactions would go a long way in building a healthy team. Organising a team party and a weekly fun friday activity may help, but that may not solve your problem.

First baby step in this journey is to introspect our actions and most importantly our reactions. This would tell us if we are acting from the here and now, or we are holding something back.This awareness would help us course correct. Fortunately for us most of us have similar patterns when it comes to conflicts, confrontations and compliments. Maintaining a journal or sharing the situation with a buddy/rubber duck, paves the way to multiple other options which we might have not thought before. The biggest step on this journey is to let go and take the plunge trusting our inner creative self.

Karthik Kamal Balasubramaniam

4.3 Are You Really Doing It?

As a Scrum Master you will be way more successful if you're doing what you expect from others, e.g.:

- If you want your team to be cross-functional and team members to be T- (or even M-) shaped, you should be a role model also in this respect.
- If you want to help your team to get better in agile by doing pair programming, test driven development, or implementing DevOps, you should be open to get better at it (or try it the first time) yourself.

Broadening your skill as a Scrum Master doesn't only mean to learn more about facilitation and coaching, it also means to learn more about what your team and your team's customer is doing. And the best way to learn all of this is by simply doing it.

And yes, most likely other team members will be better at programming, testing, and the like but, they will honor your courage to make yourself vulnerable – as they will have to make themselves vulnerable when they start working on things outside their comfort zone, entering a new domain, or learning a new technical skill.

Thus, like the other team members you are probing by running (safe) experiments yourself not by asking only others to do so. In the VUCA world (VUCA stands for volatile, uncertain, complex, ambiguous) not many of the proven (and so called best) practices work anymore, so we are all asked to probe, sense, and respond continuously. And this applies to the Scrum Master as it does to the team or the whole company (see e.g. Company-wide Agility).

As a side effect, you get a much better idea what your team really needs, where it struggles, why sometimes it takes longer to benefit from an agile technique, or why a specific agile technique is not a good fit right now, but something else is. This will make you a much better Scrum Master.

Note, that any kind of improvement starts with yourself. So get ready and start doing what you're expecting your team to do.

Jutta Eckstein

4.4 You are an informal leader – which leadership skills do you need?

Imagine the following scenario: It is a stand-up time. You are approaching the Scrum board and the whole team is already standing in front of it. Visualization of the scrum board is excellent, regardless if it is physical or digital. It is very easy to see who is working on which item and what the items are about. The flow of the items through the system is clearly understandable. The scrum team members are well prepared, no one takes more time than planned for their daily updates. The stand-up finishes on time.

Imagine now another scenario: It is a stand-up time. You have to remind people to join it. Some people are missing because they have other things to do. Visualization of the scrum board is not very good so it is not easy to understand it. The scrum team members are not well prepared with their updates so it ends up in long discussions, which are difficult to disrupt. Hence the stand-up does not finish on time. Some people get disengaged because they spent too much time on listening to something that they are not interested in. Therefore they will not join the next stand-up.

The first scenario is a dream scenario for every scrum master. How to achieve it? Well, it mainly depends on you, not only on the scrum team. As a scrum master you are an informal leader also. Regardless if your team has a development manager or an agile coach, it is you with whom the team builds respect and commitment regarding the scrum and daily stand-ups. You need the right leadership skills for building such commitment. Which skills are the most important?

In order to explain it, I'll refer to the Dr. E. Berne's Transactional Analysis theory. Berne wasn't a software engineer, but luckily for us he used a 3-layers architecture to explain how we are modeled, as persons. According to him, each of us has three ego states: Parent, Adult and Child (The so called PAC model). As the ego state's names describe, each ego state mirrors the corresponding behaviour: parent's behaviour, adult's behaviour and child's behaviour. When we are in the Parent ego state, we do as parents usually do: we are nurturing or controlling children or others. Some typical sentences coming from the parent ego state are: "Are you cold?" (nurturing) or "Listen to me now!" (controlling). The Child ego state can also be divided into two parts: The Free child - the creative and playful part of us and the Adapted child, a part of us which is accommodating and compliant. The Adult ego state is responsible for information processing and problem solving. All our communication and reactions are coming from one of these three states. Normally we are unconsciously switching between these three states all the time. But when we are aware of the PAC model, we can focus on improving our behaviours in certain situations.

Although the controlling parent sounds bad, if we take a deeper look at it, we will find that being controlling has both negative but also positive sides. While it is negative to be autocratic, fault-finding and dismissive, it is good to be structured, organised and firm, which are also a controlling parent's traits. The same applies on the nurturing parent: it has positive but also negative sides. While it is positive to be supportive and caring, it is not good to be too smothering, compassionate and overprotecting. The PAC model is presented on the Figure 1.

Figure 1 The PAC model (www.clearsay.net)

Let's take a look at the leadership skills from a PAC per-spective now. Considering all mentioned things, on which behaviours you should focus as a scrum master? People used to say that we all should be professional at work, meaning that we should mainly stay in the adult ego state. That is true. But if you want to create true engagement with the team, you also need to use your parent ego state. More correctly, you need to use positive sides of both controlling and nurturing parent states. Why and how?

First of all, you need to be well organised and structured in order to create and maintain well-structured and nicely organised daily stand-ups. You should visualise the scrum board in a good way, so that everyone can immediately understand information on it. It makes people more engaged. Also, nobody likes to waste precious time. If the daily stand-up takes just the estimated time, people will keep coming back. But be careful – do not cross the line from positive controlling to negative controlling parent state. Although you should be well planned, organised and structured you should never be critical. It will automatically disengage the team. Don't forget

- sometimes it is a thin line between keeping the structure and being critical. That is why it can be very tricky to keep staying only in the positive part of the controlling parent state.

Next, as we all know well, things do not always happen as we have planned them. People get impediments. People don't feel good when they haven't completed their tasks. People can have bad days due to many various reasons. When you see it or feel it, you should use your nurturing parent and be caring and supportive. But avoid being overprotective and smothering. Such behaviour will not help the other person. It can only create some negative behaviour in other team members.

To conclude, if you combine your professional behaviour (adult state) with just right amounts of positive controlling and positive nurturing parents states, you will be able to build the right engagement with your team. Hence, you will easily achieve the stand-up behaviour from the first scenario. Of course, you can also take a step further. You can move from having just an engaged team to something more. If you use your creative child ego state and spice your daily stand-ups with something playful and entertaining, you will create a team which is not only engaged but also really looking forward to your daily stand-ups!

Mina Boström Nakicenovic

4.5 Be like a good parent

Being a ScrumMaster is a lot like being a good parent. As a parent, you help your child to learn and grow in order to become a happy and healthy adult. Your efforts, though very big, mostly stay invisible. You see the results of all your hard work in the success of your children. When they shine, you do.

The same is true for the ScrumMaster. Your hard work makes the team shine.

Let's take this parallel a step further. We know children learn a lot from their own mistakes. So as a parent, you often face the dilemma: should I close my eyes, and let my child bump into her own mistakes? Or should I warn her, protect her, and avoid injuries?
If my 4-year old does not want to put on a coat in the winter, I will let her go outside without it. She will soon feel that it's freezing cold out there, and return asking for her coat...
But I won't let her cross a busy road by herself. I won't let her play with boiling water...

In every situation, as a good parent, I have to assess the dangers of the mistakes against the learning benefits. So that she can learn and grow, without getting seriously hurt.

The same is true for the ScrumMaster. Allow your team to make mistakes, so that they can learn. But don't let them crash.

Nicole Belilos

4.6 Stop, Collaborate and Listen...

At first glance, the following suggestions might appear to be the actions of an absent, distracted or inattentive scrummaster; however, if you look a little deeper, you will hopefully recognize that thinking about how the team reacts to these situations, actions and inactions will help you guide your team to the next level of self-organization, empowerment, collective ownership and even help mitigate that most dangerous of potential impediments...the Scrummaster !

Get team members to occasionally facilitate the retrospective. Occasionally opening the retro up to team members to facilitate can help generate new insights, allow the scrummaster to participate as a contributor, and give a new perspective on how and where the team can seek to improve. It can be extremely insightful to see the different directions that a retro can go when it's facilitated by a developer or a designer.

Skip the Stand Up.
This is a fun one, and can be really telling about how the team views the scrummaster. We hope of course that someone just kicks off the meeting as usual, but you would be surprised how often the team will wait around unsure of what to do, or even more bizarrely feel empowered to end the meeting, but not to start it!

Show all team members how to release code.
Getting code to production typically involves some level of approval, manual intervention or separation of duties (even if it's just "clicking a button"). However, this doesn't have to be the sole responsibility of the dev team members or the scrummaster. Having as many people as possible on the team aware and authorised to release to production helps grow the sense of collective ownership for the product and minimizes potential bottlenecks to delivering value.

Don't open the next ticket/request/record.
All too often the scrummaster can default into a team admin/secretary. While it is important for a scrummaster to be helpful and add value, consistently performing these tasks can create a black box scenario where no one else knows or

understands the background process required to perform an essential activity. Don't do the next one, note the knowledge gaps in the team and set about correcting the deficit.

Don't speak at the next planning session.
This potentially applies to many situations, but it traces back to the old saying, we have two ears and one mouth so we can listen twice as much as we speak. Being present, aware and engaged in a planning session adds value. Being overly forceful, filling rather than leveraging the awkwardness of silence, and driving rather than navigating, robs the teams opportunity to explore, discuss and discover new ways of working.

Get the whole team involved in acceptance testing.
Similar to releasing code, often acceptance testing becomes the responsibility of one person. Expanding this activity to the whole team increases the sense of responsibility the team has for the value they are delivering. It also increases empathy for the user and a better appreciation for what each domain within the team does.

Stay out of the Tools for a few days.
For some scrummasters it can be easy to get caught up in a world of metrics and monitoring. Tools can make this all the more alluring; however this can lead to a situation where we can't see the forest for the trees. Sure, measures like cycle time and even velocity can be useful for helping the team improve certain aspects of their work. But there is more to a team than stats and numbers. Drucker said it best, "culture eats strategy for breakfast". Every now and then forget the metrics and take some time to observe the team as they go about their day, how they interact, what makes them tick, what annoys them, and what do they like. In most cases a happy team is a productive team, the reverse is not necessarily true and ultimately is not

sustainable.

I hope you find these tips useful and would love to hear how they have worked for you, or how you have improved upon them. Feel free to reach out let me know on twitter @agileterry

Terry Harmer

4.7 How Act Is More Important Than What You Say You Believe

Every executive will freely tell anyone that will listen that they are in favor of quality, collaboration, transparency, and agility. Unfortunately, every coach or change agent runs into excuses that the organization will need to mature or the culture change before those concepts can universally translate into behavior.

A significant amount of transformation and leadership literature and practices centers on establishing or changing the culture by getting leaders to express agile values.

Instant problem.

Culture is a nebulous concept, there are two common threads in most definition values and behaviors.

Many coaches espouse value-centric definitions believing values proceed behavior.

This decision causes them to focus their efforts on getting leaders to express new values in order to change the culture. Values that often were at odds with those that propelled them up the corporate ladder.

These change programs are immediately starting in a difficult position.

Values are amorphous.

Every individual interprets specific values differently.

For example, I asked several friends to define creativity.

Each person had a different definition. Some of the differences were more than mere nuances.

Our individual interpretations would make the outcome of embracing the value of creativity unpredictable. The variability of how we interpret values that make it difficult to create a common vision and then elicit a common outcome.

Diversity makes this issue even more problematic. As someone schooled in the need for measurement and feedback, the lack of a clear definition makes monitoring and measuring a change in the values at best difficult and often outside of the expertise of most internal measurement groups.

Without a clear definition and without a mechanism for monitoring change, talking about values is merely window dressing.

While values are important, a better approach for leaders and practitioners is to focus on behaviors.

Michael Fester in his interview in the Corner Office column in the New York Times[1], "Values are ambiguous, behaviors are explicit."

Define the future state of the culture in terms of how people should behave.

How an individual behaves is a direct representation of their

---

[1]https://www.nytimes.com/2017/04/28/business/mike-oneill-bmi-leadership.html?mcubz=3&_r=0

interpretation of the values they hold.
Observed behavior can be coached, what someone believes is not easily coach-able.

As part of any change, large or small, clearly identify how people will behave as a result of any change.
Leaders must act in a manner that supports the change (they need to walk the talk).
Leaders have the further burden of holding others to account for how they behave when it conflicts with how the behaviors needed to support the change. An organization that wants to promote the value of empowerment must identify the behaviors that define empowerment, execute those behaviors, hold everyone accountable, and measure the results.

When change is required, outside of the true believers, behavior precede values, more eloquently form follows function.

Values are the focus of many changes journey.
Lofty goals are set for values such as empowerment without a linkage to behaviors.
The lack of linkage to behaviors often leads to failed change efforts.

In the end, leaders must understand that action speaks louder than words.
A leader needs to stop talking about values and rather talk about how they want the organization to behave.

Behaviors are a more accurate representation of the values being promoted.

Tom Cagley

4.8 The value of reverie

Sometimes doing nothing is the right thing to do. Especially when your goal is 'helping others do it'.

Like many before me, I learned this the hard way, and more than once. In my eagerness to get things done and done right, I do them myself, or make sure others do it "properly".

Rarely this is the kind of 'helping' required by an agile coach.

There are many kinds of helping, and one of them requires doing nothing. Instead, by letting yourself drift away you can begin listening to unspoken words. This is an art and a craft to be learned and mastered. In the words of Harrison Owen, developer of Open Space Technology[2], it's a form of being "totally present and absolutely invisible".

Begin with silently collecting evidence: Who's talking more than others? Who's not talking? Towards which groups is the culture biassed? Often programmers get more airtime than testers and men get more airtime than women. Which groups get more airtime in your culture? Which groups get more exhibits of respect? Who gets exhibits of disrespect?

Then begin asking yourself - what is the meaning of these data? What hypotheses can you make? What evidence can support or refute your hypothesis?

A wonderful practice I learned from Tova Averbuch[3], my large group facilitation teacher, is to have "a conversation with the field": During tense conversations I sometimes silently ask - "Hey, field, why is it so tense now?" Or "what is not being said

---

[2]https://en.wikipedia.org/wiki/Open_Space_Technology
[3]https://www.tovaaverbuch.com/english-home-page

right now?" And an answer usually pops within a moment or two.

Of course, having such a conversation requires to be in a state of reverie, in a kind of a day dream.

The real magic is that, besides uncovering answers you wouldn't find if you were actively talking, you also create a space for others to shine through, helping them shape their own leadership. And all you did is just being in full presence and doing virtually nothing.

Ilan Kirschenbaum

4.9 Forget about all the practices and focus on what you deliver

I started my career as a software developer in a big company following waterfall process. When Agile/Scrum was introduced to our team, we thought it's super! We didn't need to follow so many processes anymore!! We did standup meeting every day. And we tried to do a demo every 2 weeks. At the beginning, we were curious about the new way of working. And we did see the changes in team collaboration. But gradually, all the practices became routine and people got bored with it. For certain reasons we didn't like it so much as before but we don't know how to break it.

Agile means quick to adapt. If the process itself doesn't adapt according to the team's needs, then you are not agile at all.

After changing several jobs in the digital world, I found that nowadays all the development team will state that they are agile teams because they are following all the Scrum practices.

But in fact, doesn't it mean that they are delivering the work that are needed by the customer? I doubt it.

The Scrum framework itself doesn't guarantee that you make a successful delivery. From this point of view, it's no difference with the waterfall process.

If we want to make a difference when we do software projects, we should focus on what we deliver and whether we add value to our customers. When you are focusing on this goal you'll naturally have more discussion with the end users and constantly check their feedbacks. You'll naturally find the right person to do the right work without noticing whether they are cross-functional or not. And if you are trying to have long term relationship with your customer, you'll naturally focus on quality and architect. Then you'll naturally be agile.

But unfortunately, it's not a common thing in the software industry. A lot of the developers are still asking for someone to tell them what they should do. A lot of the product owners are still trying to fix the requirements with their customer. A lot of teams still don't find the right competence. The ultimate reason is that they don't care enough about what they deliver. For this, not a single practice can help.

Brenda Bao

4.10 Fool didn't know it was impossible, so she did it!

As a kid we are full of ideas, optimism, excitement, imagination, courage to follow instinct and a strong faith that anything is possible. But as we grow, we continue getting shaped from what we experience, witness, and are taught.

We learn from what we see our elders doing and believing. Subconsciously We become part of that BIG system where everything is already defined, and anyone who says, thinks or believes differently is considered a fool.

When you start your journey of an Agility Enabler (or absolutely anything else), fresh out of the training/course/certifications, you have many brilliant ideas on helping organizations/clients. But as soon as you start implementing these, you are told that your ideas are foolish and reality is different from what you think or are imagining. But isn't that the point? Reality has to be different, that is the only way we can bring the change we are imagining. We need not believe in what is already happening, only then we will be able to believe that change is possible!

Here are a few possibilities if you haven't let go of that fool inside you:

1. You will be open to learning, without ego fear or shame, because a fool doesn't know everything like an expert or wise man.
2. You will be able to selflessly serve others as a Servant leader because you are not cynical and resigned based on past bitter experiences.
3. You are able to think out of the box, innovate as are not bound by the norms.
4. You are focused on outcome rather than number of attempts or failures, hence can continue making efforts.
5. Your focus is only on the outcome and not on failures, hence you excitedly continue to experiment, inspect and adapt to improve.
6. You are always intrinsically motivated and hence aren't driven by external factors like rewards, promotion or false growth.

7. You have your own definition of growth and hence clarity on what you want to achieve.
8. You are so immersed in your journey that the opinions of others don't matter to you.

So the next question is how can someone think and operate from a 'Fool's mindset'. Here are some approaches, that you can use for self coaching as well as to coach you team/client:

1. **Come from not-knowing**: Based on our past experience, many times we give up even before starting. But what if we didn't know all of that? We would have tried and maybe made things possible. So restart with this question and then see what plan you can come up with.

2. **Be un-reasonable**: We all have our reasons for not doing things. List out all those reasons and plan considering that they do not exist. Later you can use those reasons as a Risk expert and offer strong questions that help in discovering solutions.

3. **Make friends with your inner chatter**: You inner chatter is that voice which continuously is arguing with itself on why things can happen/not-happen. It is a voice with which your logical brain warns you about things that can go wrong, resulting in limbo. Treat this voice as a friend on the other side of the phone, believing that this friend is there for you even when you fail.

4. **Laugh at yourself**: Why so serious buddy? Remember that you are but a tiny stardust participle in this endless immense universe. So lighten up, look back at your failures with a smile and gratitude for the learnings it offered, and even laugh at that epic fall.

6. **Wonder over wander**: In the world of fixed plans ensuring success, exploration and experimentation is looked upon as

wastage of time or insufficiency in knowledge. Shift your outlook from "wandering due to inexperience and wasting time" to "wondering about new possibilities".

I hope this article helped you. I wish you Fool's luck and warn you that no approach is foolproof, but then who said that everything you do will be right, and you won't fall or fail, the point is to get up and restart the journey.

Deepti Jain

5. and helping others do it.

5.1 Ask for permission

As the Scrum Master it is our job to help the team grow and develop.

A HUGE trap is to fall into "Business As Usual" and use our authority to make changes and tell people what to do. It is a very common problem. We may be even be instructed by management that we need to do this. It's our job. And we want to do our jobs so we can feel accomplishment and remain employed. So how can we proceed?

Let's pause and ask who is responsible the performance of the team? You? The team?

Remember self-organization? The only way to get to a high performing team is to have a motivated team. The way to do this is to let them own their performance. To create a space to invite them to show up in amazing ways. When we as Scrum Masters and coaches take the responsibility on, we take the responsibility away from the team. And then block the path to growth.

So what do you do?

Ask the team what they want. Ask them if they want help. Don't inflict "help" on them. That's not helpful at all. It's business as usual and acting like an oppressive boss. And it lowers performance.

Here are my favourite two questions to engage teams:
How are you performing? (1..10)
How well do you want to perform? (1..10)

If the team wants to improve, only then can you offer to help them.

Another secret of success is to repeatedly ask for permission. I suggest using one or more of: Decider Protocol[1], Fist-of-5 Decision making[2] or Advice process[3].

Michael Sahota

5.2 Helping team members to solve impediments over solving impediments themselves

Who should be handling and solving impediments? Should it be the Scrum master? The team as a whole! Their agile coach?

Leading the team and solving impediments is a full day job for many Scrum masters. Although most of them are good at it, it can drive them mad. Switching between all the different things and problems that are asking for attention doesn't feel very effective. In fact, it's hard for them to get anything done at all.

---

[1]https://liveingreatness.com/core-protocols/decider/
[2]https://agileforall.com/learning-with-fist-of-five-voting/
[3]http://agilitrix.com/2016/11/advice-process/

The Scrum guide suggests that "The Scrum Master serves the Development Team in several ways, including [...] removing impediments to the Development Team's progress". Although the Scrum master certainly plays an role when it comes to impediments, my opinion is that handling problems is a responsibility for the whole team, not only for the Scrum master.

I prefer that team members recognize and solve impediments themselves. If they see a problem, I expect team members to take action and solve it.

Scrum masters shouldn't act as firefighters. They should be developing teams, serving teams to help them improve. Coaching and mentoring team members. There's value in Scrum masters solving impediments, but it should be about teaching people how to fish instead of feeding them.

Some of the main reasons to involve team members when dealing with impediments are:

Team members other than the Scrum master might be better qualified to solve an impediment
Problems are often too complex to be solved by one person
Viewing an impediment from different angles helps to find effective solutions
Many problems have to do with the way how people work together, solving such a problem cannot be done by one person alone
You can expect from a professional that they are able to organize their work, which includes dealing with problems

You do not want the Scrum master to be a bottleneck for the team. Self organizing means that the team as a whole is capable to deal with impediments.

and helping others do it.

My tip: Prevent that the Scrum master becomes overloaded with solving impediments, involve team members when looking for solutions. Scrum masters should coach teams in finding ways to work together, and using the individual strengths of the team members when solving impediments. In this way teams can really be effective and do magic.

Ben Linders

5.3 Coaching By Listening

Have you coached a team, only to find that the advice you give falls on deaf ears? You try to help the team by offering them tips and tricks, insights and generally good advice based on your past experience. The team disagrees, actively resists or just ignores these suggestions. The next time a team won't listen to you, stop and listen to them instead!

What are the actual problems and challenges from the team's perspective? What do they think works well? What do they think needs to be improved? What are their suggestions for fixing their problems or meeting the challenges that they face? Have you heard what the team is trying to tell you or are you busy trying to make yourself heard?

Yassal Sundman

5.4 Learning is fun but can be painful

When you are a Scrum Master you sometimes find yourself in a position where you have to help people change their habits.

A change of habits is not an easy thing to do and falling back into a known habit is like slipping on a soft old shoe, that you thought you had abandoned, but that feels really nice to wear. It takes time for the brain to be re-wired and in a sense changing a habit is a lot like learning a new skill. Given a new environment or new challenges your brain is able to change itself to enable you to do what you need to be able to. But changing your brain is not without cost. It change takes effort from you and energy from the brain, and given how hard it is to learn I sometimes compare it to pain in the brain. The brain seems to want to keep things as they are, so often when you are told something you will forget it again. Even when you try it out a few times you will forget it. Even when you feel absolutely sure that this new knowledge or way of doing things is correct, your brain will often still lead you down the path it normally takes. In order to truly learn or change the brain in any other way, you need to repeat doing this new thing many times, and you need enough sleep to give the brain opportunity to change. The deep sleep removes what is not needed anymore and the light sleep drives the newly learned patterns into your brain.

How can you help as a Scrum Master? By acknowledging this, and therefore calmly and patiently repeating what they need. By explaining the why behind the new things, so that it is easier to build a pattern in the brain. By connecting it to known things to make it stick in the brain and not be removed during deep sleep. By showing by example, and speaking openly about going back to habitual thinking when things are under pressure.

Aino Corry

and helping others do it.

5.5 Silent Dotvoting

"Silence is one of the great arts of conversation"
Marcus Tullius Cicero

Dotvoting is a very popular tactic in Co-creation Land. Both on Agile Street as on Design Thinking Boulevard it is a way to converge after diverging. A way to break through endless consensus seeking discussions about what is more important. Yet there are some flaws in dotvoting which can be cured by silent dotvoting.

The general idea is quite easy. You hand out a limited number of physical round stickers and ask people to vote for items by placing a dot next to it. The alternative is - in a whiteboard setting - to ask people to draw dots with their markers.

In a serious games context, it is quite logical that humans will use game tactics. A lot of people wait for the others to put their dots first. They believe they can influence the outcome by voting at the end. Surprise, surprise, this turns out not to be the best tactic at hand.

A much more powerful effect is at play here as well. Topics that have dots on them early in the voting tend to attract more dots due to the bandwagon effect[4]. It is a wonderful example of the consensus principle as one of Cialdini's 6 principles of persuasion[5]. When people are uncertain, they will look at the behaviour of others to determine their own.

I was inspired by an article from Steve Rogalsky[6] to start using silent dotvoting. How does this work? You ask people

---

[4]https://en.wikipedia.org/wiki/Bandwagon_effect
[5]https://www.influenceatwork.com/principles-of-persuasion/
[6]http://winnipegagilist.blogspot.com/2010/11/agile-retrospectives-rising-patton.html

to write down their 3 or 5 votes on a piece of paper in silence first. You use the same mechanics as in brainwriting to avoid groupthink and ensure that everybody has a voice.

Only in a second phase, you ask people to place their dots. You can also do this as a facilitator, if the size of the group allows you to do so.

This brings a dotvoting practice to the party where you eliminate the bandwagon effect. The outcome is a more conscious and transparent way of converging, choosing and prioritizing.

Bart Vermijlen

5.6 Retrospectives are the most valuable agile practice

Retrospectives are the most valuable agile practice. Scrum Masters have a great opportunity to make the most of these by helping the team identify the biggest problem to work on, then design an experiment to make that problem smaller. As Scrum Master, make sure the team sets a SMART goal around the problem and creates a measurable hypothesis for a small experiment to work towards the goal.

Lisa Crispin

5.7 Never forget that Scrum is just as simple as chess!

A well-known saying is: "In the valley of the blind, the one-eyed man is king!". A Scrum master is in many cases that one-eyed Scrum expert in his or her environment. After all, he or she is mostly more knowledgeable than the others, and by those others often considered as the expert. A common mistake of almost any Scrum master is to overestimate his or her own knowledge about Scrum; to really think one deeply knows and understands Scrum. And if everyone else says you are the expert, before you know it you also start to believe that yourself. You start that Scrum is really simple for you.

Indeed Scrum is simple. Yes. It is just as simple as......chess! The rules of Scrum (and of chess) are easy to learn and quite fast to practice. However, both are really hard to master. You will never be done learning. I have learned (the hard way) to keep remembering myself that deeply understanding Scrum is impossible. There will always be more to discover. Just as with chess. Everyone knows that chess is very complex, despite its' simple rules. The more you master chess, the more you start to learn how difficult it is. Scrum is similar. The complexity does not lie in its rules. These are simple. The complexity of Scrum lies in using it in practice; playing the game. Adopting it in teams and organisations that consist of many different individuals, with different needs and backgrounds, and different users and customers. That makes it complex.

Using Scrum is hard. Just as hard (or maybe even harder) than chess! Never forget this. The more expertise you have on Scrum, the more you will become aware of how little you know. Grandmasters in chess are modest about their understanding of the game. So will grandmasters in Scrum become modest about their understanding. So, if you think you know it all, start looking for your blind spots.

Because if you really would know it all, you would not overestimate your own knowledge.
One thing for example is the Scrum guide. You probably have

heard about it, maybe studied it for one of the certification exams. But do you really know it? How often did you study it actually? How frequently do you still consult the Scrum guide? Do you think you know everything that is inside? Really? Do you, for example, know the Scrum values by heart? From front to back and reverse? And do you live these values and consult them in your daily decision making?

In my consulting practice I have often used the Scrum guide in trainings to build a quiz. I let participants come up with multiple choice questions directly based on it. This provides excellent exercising for the Scrum.org exams too, by the way. In such a quiz, the participants build exam questions for each other, directly based on the Scrum guide text. I then acted as judge and jury during the quiz itself, in case of doubt. And I thought I knew it all! But to be really frank, in about every 5 questions I had to take the Scrum guide and check things. Because there is so much detail in the guide that you will never really understand Scrum by reading it once or twice. After a few of these quizes, I gained even greater respect for Jeff Sutherland and Ken Schwaber. Every word in the guide has a reason. Every sentence is there with a purpose. I often was surprised by the things I learned during such a training quiz. Upfront I often thought Scrum did not have surprises for me, but I was wrong. Many times!

So my tip to every Scrum master is to consider Scrum just as simple as chess. That means you should never overestimate your personal knowledge, and try to remain modest towards your own expertise regarding Scrum. Yes, you may have years of experience. Yes, you may be the guru in your organisation. Yes, you have written numerous blogs, articles or maybe even books about it. Still, there is so much hidden between the lines. You never stop learning in chess. The same holds for Scrum.

Rini Vansolingen

5.8 Zoom Out

Have you heard the expression "context is king"? It's very true if you work with teams because many of the things that can affect a team negatively can be found outside of the team itself. How good is your understanding of your team's context?

When the world around our teams is messy, it's natural to latch onto the smaller and local, team specific, questions and shield ourselves from the complexity that surrounds us. In the worst case, we end up with a powerful "illusion of progress": we work hard and efficiently in our own bubble, but ultimately we fail anyway.

Obviously, a team should focus on doing its job but if a team focuses too much inwards it looses touch with the reality it exists in. Doing team work well means taking good care both of the internals of the team and the context the team is operating in. The context is what informs about what solution to develop, and why. It also contains the resources and support we need to succeed. So, we'd better understand it well.

Some years ago I learned an exercise we can use to help our teams build situational awareness, but before we dive into the practice of doing this, I want to explore why understanding "the bigger picture" is so important for successful collaboration.

Whenever we try to collaborate in an organization, we experience different kinds of friction. We resist, argue, and misunderstand each other. Without shared understanding it's very hard to pull in the same direction.

Don't fall into the trap of believing that others disagree with with you out of stupidity or ill will. That happens of course, but in my experience people are trying to do what makes sense, from their point of view. The question is what their point of view really is? If we knew that, we would understand others better and be better able to collaborate - or intelligently discuss - with them. We may not accept their worldview, but we might be able to understand it better.

So without further ado, here is an exercise I use to rapidly build new insight in groups. I first learned this from Jerry Weinberg who called this technique org mapping. I believe he was inspired by Virginia Satir's family mapping. The idea is to visualize a bit of the context around a group of people, so that their understanding and empathy can deepen. One caveat: it's quite easy to do this, but it can shake out uncomfortable truths quickly, so make sure you are ready to handle whatever comes up.

Having gathered a group of people, I begin by handing out blank sheets of paper (larger is often better) and various colored pens, including black ones. I explain that we'll be doing some doodling in order to better understand their situation.

Participants to begin by writing out a question about the situation that they want to explore - this often creates focus and gives clarifies the motivation for completing this slightly silly exercise.

At this point, I also point out that the aim here is not to create aesthetically pleasing works of art. We'll be creating visual models of real situations, and as long as we get something to point at and reason about, they are perfect.

I then instruct participants to add the things in the list below.

and helping others do it.

We add one theme at a time with just a few minutes spent on each:

1. Draw yourself (in the middle, and not too large, and a simple stick figure is fine)
2. Add other people (or groups, roles, organizations etc)

Here I ask people to use size and placement so that their pictures seem reasonable. For example, some people might need to be really small and far away, and others larger and close by.

3. Add things (products, documents, hardware, buildings, ...)

Again, scale and place things as makes sense. Remember that we don't need to add everything, just the things that make the model useful to us. I emphasize that it will be useful for participants to zoom out one step more than they usually do, when thinking about this situation. For example: who are the customers of our customers, and what do we really know about them?

1. Draw interactions (information flows, relationships, bound-aries, ...). For these I explain that arrows of different kinds are useful, as are circles and other lines of various thicknesses and styles.

The pictures are probably getting a bit messy by now. Using different colors can help.

Next, things get a lot more exicting. Now we are ready to start adding opinions about what it is like to actually be in the depicted situation. So, in turn, we add:

5. Problems (everything from a little friction to major crises)
6. Strengths (things we want to keep building on)
7. Other things that need to go in the picture

As you can imagine you can do a lot of interesting variations or changes to this exercise. You could add other categories to help catalyze ideas: who has power, who thinks or says what, which informal alliances exist, and so on.

When I participated in this with Jerry Weinberg some years ago, he ended by asking us to give our drawings a title. I really like how this causes us to externalize and summarize so this is how I usually end the drawing too. Don't be surprised if the titles of your paintings contain some variant of the word "mess".

In fact, the word "mess" is the exact term that systems thinker Russell Ackoff used to describe the interacting system of problems that characterize organizations. I love how clearly we see just how complex our workplaces are whenever we draw them like this. Again, we are not assuming that we are looking at reality here, just one quick attempt at sketching out one perspective on it. I call this kind of work "zooming out".

So what do we do with these drawings? We explore them together in dialogue, with the explicit purpose of better understanding the perspective of others. We explore the interactions that produce the performance of this organization. By combining our various perspectives on a situation, we approximate a more true understanding of the reality we find ourselves in.

A word of caution. Zooming out can awaken feelings of hopelessness. Large organizations in particular always come with an unhealthy serving of institutionalized insanity. Seeing this and realizing how hard it will be to change is tough. Still, we need to do what we can, here and now. We dig where we stand. Understanding the larger picture can help us make meaningful local changes, even we currently lack the formal power to change the system at large. With a better understanding of the larger whole, we might even be able to start to influence it more effectively.

Tobias Fors

5.9 Support the interactions between individuals

As humans, we need to connect with other people. It's in our make-up. If we don't get the support we need through these connections, then we can become demotivated and disengaged.

Organisations are people and people need support systems.

If people feel like their organisation isn't supporting them, this can actually feel like rejection. Which is terrible for morale, and in turn is not great for making excellent products.

Being supported means: feelings of belonging; help when it's needed; autonomy to make decisions; free to take opportunities, and time to develop.

Teams often have this; they support each other and become a tight-knit unit. But we can't forget cross-team collaboration, people in different locations or those that aren't in teams.

Individuals need opportunities to interact with each other

meaningfully. Through social activities, collaborative learning, knowledge sharing and collaboration.

If you are working in a team, create opportunities and a regular habit of interacting with others.

If you are working across teams or organisations, find ways to make this part of the culture. Set up communities of practice, communities of interest or collaborative working groups.

And don't forget about yourself, find ways to connect with other people who can support you.

Emily Webber

5.10 It's not just the question you ask, but how you ask it!

I recall a moment at an Agile conference in Bangkok where I had the pleasure of sitting next to an American agile coach that had just started working for a client there a few months ago. Our conversation meandered around the topics presented at the conference, our backgrounds and what brought us to the same event. I ask her the same question I ask any western coach working in Asia, "So, what do you see that's different here?" Her reaction was immediate, she blurted out "Why don't Asians speak up? Why don't they answer my questions? I find myself speaking most of the time to what feels like a blank wall."

If you ever had this kind of interaction with a team, then you might be in the same proverbial boat:

> Me: Alright team, what can we improve on for the next
> sprint?
> Them: *silence*
> Me: Anyone? I would appreciate some sharing.
> Them: *more silence*
> Me: Ok, is there anything?
> Them: *Even more silence....*

Usually someone will speak up at this point, but it would usually be the same person that spoke up last time...

I hear similar stories from western coaches, managers and expats working in Asia. I calmly replied, "Well, it's not just the question you ask, it's how you ask it. When people don't answer, it doesn't mean that they don't have anything to say, it could mean that they just don't know how to deliver you that answer."

Many Asian cultures pride speaking with intention and deliberation, to give mindful answers. Doing so requires time and space for reflection. This is in direct contrast to the expectation to just speak up and reply instantaneously. Consider creating space for thought, give people time to think and form their responses. Give them post-its and markers to write down their responses.

Here's how the conversation could go differently by changing the mode of response.

> Me: Alright team, what can we improve on next time?
> I'll give you all a few minutes to form your response. Feel

free to jot it down on the post-its provided.
Them: *scribbles away*
Me: Times up, I see that most of you had written something down. Let's spend some time sharing our thoughts with each other. Could someone please start?

By giving people the time, space and opportunity, we are more likely to receive meaningful responses, particularly from thoughtful, introspective people. So the next time you feel that people "don't speak up," consider that it could be how you're asking the question!

Tze Chin Tang

5.11 Let's talk about the p-word.

Understanding privilege is key to becoming a better ally. At its core, privilege is a set of unearned benefits given to people who fit into a specific social group. Due to our race, class, gender, sexual orientation, language, geographical location, ability, religion and more, all of us have greater or lesser access to resources and social power.

People who are marginalized in multiple ways experience amplified marginalization and drastically reduced privilege. This is due to intersectionality, the fact that the combination of someone's identities creates an intersection of overlapping and compounded oppressions.I appreciate this example by Kittu Pannu, who wrote about intersectionality in the LGBT community for Impakter:

and helping others do it.

> One could assume that a black, queer woman would, in essence, have a more difficult life experience than a heterosexual white male just by virtue of her experiences as a woman, compounded with her experience as a black person, and topping it off with her queer identity. Her life will be just a little harsher, her earning potential just short of the people around her, her ability to say with certainty that she gets everything she deserves not as strong as a white male's ability. She would have to work that much harder to be taken seriously in today's heteronormative, white, male-dominated world.

The term intersectionality was originally coined by Kimberlé Crenshaw in her 1989 essay "Mapping the Margins: Intersectionality, Identity Politics, and Violence against Women of Color,"[7] and she explores it further in her excellent TED talk, "The Urgency of Intersectionality."[8] In nearly all cases, being marginalized in multiple ways leads to diminished privilege and increased risk of discrimination and violence.

Now, here's where it gets tricky: Privilege is often invisible to those who have it. This means that many people get defensive when someone points out their privilege. It's tempting to think of privilege as being associated with extreme unearned advantages like having a massive family trust fund or being related to some influential person. Having one's privilege pointed out might feel like the equivalent of being told that one is lazy, lucky, or undeserving of good things — or that one's life has been easy. Many people are quick to respond

---

[7] https://www.jstor.org/stable/1229039

[8] https://www.ted.com/talks/kimberle_crenshaw_the_urgency_of_intersectionality?language=en

that they've had their fair share of difficulties and faced down prejudices too.

But doing this means forgetting that privilege is simply a system of advantages granted to all people in a given group. It's a social structure that has become endemic to human cultures. It's not about who you are as an individual as much as it is about which groups you belong to and how those groups are viewed and treated by society. A person isn't privileged because of being a rotten, freeloading bum; They're privileged because they're white or middle-class or cisgender.

Being privileged doesn't mean you've never worked hard, and it doesn't necessarily mean that your life has been easy. Here's a fabulous analogy from Sian Ferguson via the website Everyday Feminism[9]:

> Let's say both you and your friend decide to go cycling. You decide to cycle for the same distance, but you take different routes. You take a route that is a bit bumpy. More often than not, you go down roads that are at a slight decline. It's very hot, but the wind is at [sic] usually at your back. You eventually get to your destination, but you're sunburnt, your legs are aching, you're out of breath, and you have a cramp.
>
> When you eventually meet up with your friend, she says that the ride was awful for her. It was also bumpy. The road she took was at an incline the entire time. She was even more sunburnt than you because she had no sunscreen. At one point, a strong gust of wind blew her over and she hurt her foot. She ran out of water halfway through. When she hears about your route, she remarks that your experience seemed easier than hers.

_____

[9]https://everydayfeminism.com/

> Does that mean that you didn't cycle to the best of your
> ability? Does it mean that you didn't face obstacles? Does
> it mean that you didn't work hard? No. What it means is
> that you didn't face the obstacles she faced.

Privilege doesn't mean your life is easy or that you didn't
work hard. It simply means that you don't have to face the
obstacles others have to endure. It means that life is more
difficult for those who don't have the systemic privilege you
have.

Look at any business segment, and you'll find people who
have more privilege than others. In today's tech industry, they
tend to be straight, white men. Perhaps they attended highly
selective universities such as Stanford, MIT, or an Ivy League
school. They may have strong networks of people in similar
positions of privilege. They are the majority.

Yet privilege is not limited to straight, white guys.

I'm white, straight, and able-bodied, which means I have a
lot of privilege myself. I hold a degree in computer science
from Brown University. I'm a published author and a TEDx
speaker. Formerly, I was a vice president of a well-known
tech company. Yup. That's a lot of privilege. And my experience is a great reminder that people who are members of
systematically oppressed groups (such as women) can still
have privilege due to their membership in other groups (such
as being white straight, etc.)

This excerpt was adapted from Better Allies: Everyday Actions to Create Inclusive, Engaging Workplaces.[10] Copyright

---

[10]https://betterallies.com/

Karen Catlin

6. Through this work we have come to value

6.1 Why and How to Claim Wins For Personal and Team Power

If you want to be a winner--and if you want to be on a winning team--then get in the
habit of winning every day. The practice of claiming wins and celebrating them together

- grants us permission to win
- reveals our intentions to ourselves and others, and
- supports our acknowledgment of each other's power to generate wins.

Adopt this definition of a Win:something you intend to happen does happen, or
something you intend not to happen doesn't happen.
Note that a win is not a size. It is an intention met. Most of us are expert at noticing --
and claiming -- the frustrations of life. We moan, snipe, roll our eyes, etc. That's losing.
So we expect to experience more of it, and sure enough, we

69

do.

It's what we are filtering for.

So start by yourself. Identify five wins from yesterday. Don't edit ("Nah, that one wasn't

big enough." Stop it!). Just name five intentions met.

- I meant to thank my team yesterday for a great demo and I did. Win.
- I intended to write that challenging letter yesterday and I did. Win.
- I intended to not get sick yesterday and I didn't. Win.
- …

That wasn't so hard.

Now, put a reminder on your smart device to think of five, ten, or maybe twenty wins

from yesterday first thing every morning right after you get up. Then do it.

Then, introduce Wins to your teams. Experiment with adding one win per person to your

stand up. If it doesn't fit well at the daily meeting, then at most of your other meetings, at

the beginning, to set the tone of winning.

Consider this: It's a good meeting when we have so many wins there is no time for

problems.

And remember, don't step on anyone's win! If it's their win, it's their win. Say

Congratulations. That's what we naturally say to each other when reporting wins.

Christopher Avery

6.2 Know the Work

Almost every team I meet has the same problem: too much Priority #1 work.

They have at least one project's worth of features stuffed into their iteration. Often, they're attempting to work on two or three projects at "one time," along with some variety of support. They might do Customer Support, Production Support, Sales Support—whatever it is, it's not features.

Some teams try the "everyone take their own story" approach, a form of multitasking. That doesn't work because—at some point—the team members have to collaborate to complete something.

Other teams try to rank the work once and for all—and a HiPPO (Highest Paid Person's Opinion) changes their ranking. Changing the ranking turns into another form of multitasking.

Multitasking doesn't work.

In reality, we fast-switch. And, since we aren't computers, we lose state and then make mistakes. We need an alternative.

How can you know what your team is doing? Write it down.

Don't just write the work down in a tool. Write it down on paper. I prefer cards—yes, index cards—on the wall. Stickies work, too.

Here's why I prefer paper: The tool swallows the work, never showing the team they have accepted the work or that the work now creates too much to do.

I have a guideline for my work and for the work I do with teams:

> Don't accept work until someone writes that work
> down on a card and puts that card on a board.

When your team uses a physical board, the team—and the people who want to add to the team's work—will soon see that the board is full or even past capacity. Paper cards help hold the team's capacity to the number of cards on the wall that will fit on the board.

The team sees several benefits from writing the work down:

- No one tries to hold that information in their heads. David Allen says, "Your head is a lousy office." If we're busy thinking about work to do, we're not thinking about the work we're doing.
- Everyone can see that the team has added work to the board—often, unanticipated work. That helps everyone see "why" the team hasn't finished what they expected to finish.
- No one can push work to the team without writing a card. That means no email, voicemail, or chat requests. The team needs a card.

Until everyone can see all the work, the team will feel pushed and pulled into more work. When everyone can see the work, the team and other interested people, can rank it. Until then, the team will thrash like crazy.

Leaders don't let teams thrash.

Johanna Rothman

6.3 How To Reduce Groupthink In remote Meetings

Individuals often make bad decisions. We buy things we don't need. We eat things we know we shouldn't. So at work, we often get together to share decision-making, in the hope that since two heads are better than one, many heads should make great decisions.

But the research shows that groups often make worse decisions than their individual members! (See Reid Hastie and Cass Sunstein's book, Wiser[1].)

'Groupthink' is the technical name for this phenomenon – the dysfunctional decision-making of a group of people deliberating together. You have groupthink when the value of the group is less than the sum of its parts.

Research has highlighted four specific varieties of groupthink:

Groups don't just fail to correct members' mistakes, they amplify them
Group members tend to follow those who speak first: the 'cascade effect'
Groups tend to become more polarised and extreme than their individual members
Groups focus on what everyone knows and miss out on information that may be held by only one member.
Here are five proven strategies to counteract groupthink in a meeting:

Listen to, and acknowledge, what people say. Use their words! Make sure everyone speaks early in a meeting

---

[1]https://www.amazon.co.uk/dp/B00O4CRR9C

Leaders speak last!

Invite difference. Separate divergent and convergent phases of discussion.

Ask lots of non-judgemental questions to tease out different opinions and uniquely-held knowledge.

How does all of this relate to remote meetings? The truth is that the way people typically behave in remote meetings can make groupthink worse – even when people think they are 'doing the right thing'.

For example, people tend to want to make online meetings as short as possible. That's efficient, right?

Well, no. Looking through a groupthink lens, the quickest way to finish a meeting with 'agreement' is for the leader to speak first, invite clarifying questions, then everyone agrees with him and the meeting ends. In fact, why bother to have a meeting at all? The leader could just send an email.

This information-update is the very lowest level of conversation[2]. It has its place, but it's not conducive to effective joint decision-making.

Technology used to restrict our ability to have more sophisticated, creative, collaborative conversations remotely, but that's not the case nowadays. Almost all our best facilitation techniques, such as Liberating Structures[3], can work when you use a good-quality video-conferencing platform. Breakout rooms, for example, allow for the separation of divergent discussions.

What needs to happen to upgrade your online conversations! How might you use the five strategies for reducing groupthink?

---

[2]https://judyrees.co.uk/5-tips-for-higher-quality-conversations/
[3]http://www.liberatingstructures.com/

Judy Rees

6.4 Becoming Comfortable with Being Uncomfortable

Have you ever been to the Venetian Hotel in Las Vegas? They have performers dressed like Italian statues, who stand absolutely still for hours atop pedestals while people pose and take pictures with them, and leave tips at their feet. What a terribly difficult and uncomfortable job!

Those rock solid performers, with their grace, steadfastness, and ability to withstand discomfort day after day, make me think of ScrumMasters. In my CSM classes I always start with how important it is for ScrumMasters to learn how to become comfortable with being uncomfortable. It sounds like an oxymoron, but the simplicity of this simple phrase was a guiding notion in my development and still holds true for me today, almost two decades later.

ScrumMasters, dissuade yourself of the notion that if you know what you are doing and are doing the job right, then it will be easy and there will be no discomfort. That's rubbish! It's rarely comfortable for anyone to speak in front of groups, deliver bad news, facilitate a dysfunctional team meeting, or mediate a difficult dispute – even when we have the skills to do the job and years of experience. Yet many of us do this work with confidence, making it appear as if we are feeling quite comfortable. This does not mean that we are, nor does it mean that it's easy. It's hard work; but speaking personally, my discomfort helps me to stay alert and focused.

I once gave a keynote at an agile conference. At the end of my keynote there was a wonderful teaching moment where

everyone got to observe and experience what I meant by
learning to become comfortable with being uncomfortable.
I left the stage and went out into the audience and asked
if anyone would like to share their agile stories, and I was
met with silence. I stood there and smiled, waiting, while
everyone stared at me, the silence stretched out. Everyone
was becoming very uncomfortable, including me! But I knew
someone would eventually say something – someone always
does – and lo and behold, there was a volunteer in the back.
His sharing opened the floodgates, and soon hands were up
around the room.

So experiment with the art of being comfortable with being
uncomfortable. Put yourself in some uncomfortable, but safe,
situations and see what happens. Ask a question and hold the
silence like a gift – I promise you someone will eventually say
something! The more you see how things turn out fine, the
more comfortable you'll come to be with your discomfort.

Michele Sliger

6.5 Curiosity Over Judgment

This seems a simple way-of-being sort of thing to include in
tips for scrum masters in an agile context, and I suppose it is.
When it was recommended to me by Alex Harms some time
ago it was a formulation of something I'd been striving for
over several years.

When we are in any system and know the rules and principles
of the system, we tend to have expectations. Maybe our
expectation is about scrum rituals (such as 15 minute daily
scrums) or definition of done. Maybe it is about the kinds of
conversations we should have. Perhaps we expect certain XP

practices to be followed. Maybe we expect more management support and respect.

The trigger point for this idea is when we feel that the situation is wrong: Reality is not meeting our expectations, people are doing the wrong things, the metrics are disappointing, we don't see the emotions and attitudes we expect.

So, don't judge the moment. It's not wrong, even if it's unwanted. When expectations and reality are not aligned, consider which one of the two is true. If we didn't predict and expect it, it is because something happened that wasn't in our intention. That's just data.

What is different? What can we learn from it?

The difference between expectations and reality is a curiosity space. It has much to teach us if we don't refuse and reject its lessons. Sometimes the best things that have happened in my career came from examining this curiosity space.

If you are open to it, the world has many things to teach you as a coach, scrum master, manager, or team member. Don't close yourself off by judging the world you didn't expect as "wrong."

Go investigate and grow.

Tim Ottinger

6.6 Letting Go

I am a bit of a worrier and an overachiever. My brain forever mulling over the next plan, the next equation, the next problem, wanting to get it right, improve, do better than last time.

While this characteristic has served me well in my career, and in life, my personal improvement backlog, if printed on letter sized paper and taped together end to end, would stretch halfway to the moon. Sometimes it's a bit too much.

Many years ago I had put a lot of pressure on myself to make every retrospective completely different. I pored over books, read online articles, talked to friends, scoured the earth for new ideas. You see, I had somehow landed at the conclusion that I would be a facilitation failure if I ran the same retrospective format more than once in a year. Well, my team at the time, who were aloof, really smart guys, not very eager to get in touch with their emotional sides, and all business, needed a new format, I decided, so I unveiled the Emotions Seismograph in their next retrospective. The fits of nervous laughter from my team completely derailed the point of the exercise. People were drawing all over the place, making a joke out of it, discussing nothing but how foolish the exercise was. I realized afterward that I had become so caught up in "improvement" that I forgot momentarily about the most important thing of all: the needs of the people on my team and what may or may not have resonated with them. I forgot to meet them where they were.

It isn't always helpful for a person like me living in this 'tips and tricks'-oriented world. That is, type your favorite challenge into a web browser and you'll get articles, blogs, and YouTube videos on what to try next. It's not a bad thing, at all; it's rather wonderful that people can help each other. After all, I suspect that you're a ScrumMaster because of the possibility of improvement, among other things, and you're probably very interested on how to improve. That's great!

Sometimes... well, sometimes you just need to step away from the laundry list of tips, the incessant consultant buzzword references that can leave you feeling lost and unschooled, facilitation patterns for this and that, etc., and just get back to the basics. Connect with the team in whatever way feels natural, maybe in a way that didn't come from a book (yes, I realize the irony of reading this in a book J). Let a sprint pass in which you're not hyper-focused on improving everything. Breathe. Remember that there is a next sprint. A person can very easily get caught up in trying so hard, so much, for so long that they end up burning out.

And you, my dear ScrumMaster, we need you to never burn out.
Stacia Viscardi

6.7 Introverts on Agile teams, and how small changes can make a big difference

I am an introvert. Somewhere between 30 and 50% of humans self identify as such. In the software industry, my guess is that there are even more of us. But how does this go together with Agile? Does this large number of introverts mean that Agile is bound to fail, or at least make us all miserable? No, not really, and I am going to tell you why, but first a disclaimer; even though Introversion is a personality trait, a part of our personality that is relatively fixed over time, it is as I like to call it one dimension of our personality, and one of many. Just as every person is different, every introvert or extrovert is different, or as Brian of Nazareth puts it; You are all individuals... you are all different.[4] '' Yes, even you who

---

[4] https://www.youtube.com/watch?v=QereR0CViMY

just said that you're not. Some things I say on this page might fit you and your views of introversion, and some might not.

With that out of the way, let me start by giving you my view of Introversion and in order to do this I will need to compare it to extraversion. An important point to make is that introversion shall not get mixed up with shyness. Being shy means to have a fear of social judgement and has nothing to do with introversion. In the simplest terms, in the most convenient definitions an introvert gets drained from socializing while an extrovert gains energy from the same. This leads to introverts preferring a smaller group of friends. They prefer spending time alone rather than going out on a friday night. They dislike attention and are often much quieter at meetings or other gatherings. They are often good listeners and have a strong attention to detail, but will frequently keep their ideas to themselves. Most introverts are not very competitive. They also run a high risk of suffering from The Introvert Hangover as Susan Cain calls it in her great book Quiet[5] . The Introvert Hangover is a state where you have completely drained yourself and will need several hours (or days) of solitude in order to bounce back.

To make matters even more complicated, there's not just one type of introversion. Professor Jonathan Cheek of Wellesley College and his colleagues have come up with the STAR-model of introversion[6] which defines four types of introversion. Social, Thinking, Anxious and Restrained. I will not go into details of the model here, but if you are interested I advice you to look it up, it is somewhat of an
eye-opener. What is important to know is that every introvert

---

[5]https://www.amazon.com/Quiet-Power-Introverts-World-Talking-ebook/dp/B0074YVW1G/

[6]https://www.academia.edu/7353616/Four_Meanings_of_Introversion_Social_Thinking_Anxious_and_Inhibited_Introversion

(or human being for that matter) has these four types of introversion to some extent and hence we are all different. Me for instance, I score quite high on social and thinking introversion but not very high on restrained. You will score differently.

Making everyone awesome

So how come introverts choose to be on agile teams? I believe that much of it comes down to motivation. We are all motivated to do a good job, and I for one believe that collaborating with others in teams might just be the best way to do that. You can however make working life a little bit easier for introverts by
making small adjustments with introverts in mind. Here are a few quick tips that will take you and your team a bit closer to perfection:

1. Some introverts need to refuel during the day. If they choose to work on something by

themselves for a while, let them. They are not anti-social, they might just need some time to regain the energy needed to work with others. Why not suggest lunch walks alone or in pairs.,That is an excellent way to gain vital energy for the afternoon.

2. Introverts need restorative niches, somewhere where they can be by themselves for a while.Perhaps a quiet corner of the room where they can sit with their backs against the wall. Make sure these places exists in your workplace, otherwise the introverts on your team might be left with taking long toilet breaks.

3. Some introverts are very analytical and something you might call "slow thinkers". Let activities that require deep thinking take time if needed. An example might be brainstorming. Instead of scheduling a meeting to brainstorm around something, post the question on a flipchart where people often pass e.g. on their way to the water cooler and let them post suggestions at their own pace. Let it take a few days. This also helps people to refuel their creative process by reading what others have posted. The same goes for retrospectives. Send the subject of the retrospective to all attendants prior to the meeting, allowing them to reflect and gather some data ahead of the actual retrospective.

4. Use mob programming. In fact, empirical evidence shows that mob programming works very well for introverts. It is easy to jump in and out of a mob if you need a break, and everyone can contribute at their own pace. Just make sure that people have a way to let the mob know they have an idea that they need to process for a while before sharing it with the rest of the group.

5. Work hard to make your work environment safe. Members who feel safe are more prone to share their thoughts and ideas. People can also be themselves in a safe team and can spend their energy on doing an awesome job instead of playing roles. In the end, that is why we are there.

Finally I have a bonus tip if your team is sitting in an open space environment:

6. Get a team room. At least make sure that your team can sit at the same place every day,

because if you are stuck with hotdesking, chances are that the introverts on your team will leave, or even worse, get burned out before you know it.

Tobias Anderberg

6.8 Craft Experiences Not Arguments

When one reads the phrase, "...through this work we have come to value...", we tend to sweep right past it to get to the good part: what we've come to value. I see it differently, and in particular, I want to highlight the extreme urgency of "through this work".

Our movement is about change, in code, in individuals, in teams. I am a professional software development coach, a specialist in fomenting change. Because I'm reasonably good at that, people often ask me how I do it, what my secret is, for helping at the birth of change.

My secret: **Craft experiences, not arguments**.

We come to value ideas, process, or techniques, by experiencing them in play. All the words in the world can't tell you how to ride a bicycle, and they also can't begin to capture what riding a bicycle feels like, especially how *good* it feels, in so many dimensions at once.

- Do a two-hour mob on a kata.
- Do a two-week stretch of "pull & swarm" instead of scrum.
- Try promiscuous pairing for half a day for a week.

- Take a single file in your codebase and bring it under perfect TDD & Refactoring discipline.

When you do this, when you re-center your approach to change around creating experiences, you dramatically increase the likelihood of success. And arguments don't go away, but they shift focus to become far easier, because they're not about "from now on", they're about "let's try this is in a safe place for a short time".

If you like these agile ideas, if you want to spread them in your team, think hard about what you will have to do to create the experiences people use to change. The shortest route to deep change is the one captured in just these words:
through this work we have come to value ...

Michael Hill

6.9 Slow Down, then Speed up

When I'm invited to coach an agile transformation, the general ask of me is: "Please fix the teams. They aren't delivering fast enough. I thought this Agile thing was supposed to be faster and better."
That's partially true if you take care to get the foundation right. However, it's a falsehood if you're applying process control under the guise of Agile – you may see some improvement, but nothing close to what is possible.

For me, Agile or any new way of working, has been like learning how to dance. I took dance lessons as an adult for eight years – I learned how to foxtrot, tango, and salsa my way around a dance floor. That journey began in preparation for my then upcoming wedding. We asked a studio to make us great swing dancers, so we would feel and look amazing for our first dance. After much discussion, we were told they would not make us awesome swing dancers. They would however teach us several different dance styles, with an emphasis on swing, and a basic choreographed dance for the song we had selected. We were disappointed and did not understand why we couldn't focus on the one we cared about. We followed their plan anyway.

I wasn't new to dancing when I began classes, but I felt like Bambi learning how to move all over again when lessons began. It was a slow and painful process. It was frustrating not being able to dance very well. We wanted to throw in the towel many times. I'm glad we didn't though, because we did rock our first dance to basic swing steps. Very basic - but our guests didn't know that and loved it. 15 years after my first class and many lessons later, my body moves smoothly across a dance floor without a thought required – I got my dance foundation right.

In the process of slowing down the dance, I trained not only my body, but my mind to respond differently. Steps, pivots, and movements from toes to head became second nature. The result was being able to easily adapt to the changing nature of a dance floor, flowing around others without collision, with plenty of fancy steps and twirls along the way. The truth is, I stopped dancing and became a dancer. I never would have gotten there if I hadn't slowed down first.

So about Agile... it's the same thing. You are choosing to learn a new way of working, collaborating, responding, pivoting, creating, delivering, and thinking. Agile is about agility. It requires being responsive to the changing nature and needs of customers, projects, environment, leadership, culture, and people. Especially people... because people are living breathing beings, not robots.

We slow down in part to learn the new work structures, practices, and techniques. We slow down to learn and explore so we can be better. More importantly, we slow down to shift mindset around values and beliefs. That change does not happen overnight for most of us.

People self-select to join or stay in organisations because they align with the organisational values, or the benefits of being there outweigh the conflict in values. When we choose to shift our organisation towards agility, we are also choosing to shift our values inherent in what agile means and is founded upon. That may create conflict for people. It takes time to practice these new ways of working, but it often takes longer to shift into alignment with truly agile values and beliefs. It takes practice to shift our thinking, not only our way of working.

Mindset takes time to change because we are people ingrained with decades of life-experience, with loads of practice thinking and being a certain way. This doesn't unravel overnight. It requires the right support of someone who can light the way (think a great agile leader or coach)– just like my dance teachers did for me. It requires practice working in new ways – just like practicing the same steps over and over again. It also requires patience, curiosity, and courage to embark on this new journey.

The outcome is completely worth it. The teams I've worked with who trusted me to slow down a little while to get their foundation right have reaped benefits beyond their imagining. It's how a collection of teams I worked with went from 'death row agile - aka who will be fired' to a positive example of agile working well within 3 months of coaching them. 18 months later I heard they were a stellar example of agile success throughout the multi-national company. They finally got the foundation right. They were no longer doing agile, they were being agile.

If you really want to do agile well, you have to stop doing, and start being. To do that, slow down, then speed up.

Selena Delesie

6.10 Mind the short and the long

I once worked as a Scrum Master with a Product Owner who was working very hard to acquire users and gain popularity. It got popular all right, but within a year the product was dumped in the process of corporate merger and only the brand name remained. I thought to myself, we worked for here and now but didn't think about our future enough.

In another time, I was in a Scrum team as part agile coach and part developer. The developers were all seasoned experts and generated very solid code with good automated tests. We understood maintainability is key to prolonged success. The Product Owner had produced good user stories backed by a great vision. After a year our sponsor canceled the endeavor due to the number of active users which was less than 10. You can say our development was too slow, or the product backlog didn't focus on the present enough. Either way, I can safely assume that we failed to satisfy the people in time.

Agile is about prolonged success, which means your team needs to deliver value in the present AND in the future. You need to survive now to make a future. You need to make your ground better now or you'll see a diminished future.

- Team needs to implement a working feature in current sprint,
- and team needs to refactor code for future sprints

- Product Owner should choose PBIs to satisfy stakeholders now,
- and PO should choose PBIs to satisfy users in the future

- The team is crucial for the current product to be successful,
- and the same team needs to work on a future innovation for the company to thrive

Two basic points to win in the long
Simplicity is an obvious thing to be done now for the future. You should incorporate just enough complexity, which yields the most simple solution to the current problem, to be able to adapt to unexpected events in the future. To make the present product as simple as possible now, you need to refactor, modify, or remove functionalities from the product aggressively.

Another point is to have a vision, and The Product Goals described in The Scrum Guide 2020. Your plan and product backlog will become an endless path toward perfecting the vision, guided by the goals as milestones, starting right at the front of the present with an item which must be done now. Also let them dictate how to survive by paying the bills and make the team happy enough in the coming sprints.

Start with a plan. Continue with refined plans.
You start with a plan when you're doing waterfall. You start with a plan when you're agile. The difference is in how you

handle the plan – you keep changing the plan to adapt to reality. So you always know what must be done to progress by realizing a top fraction of the plan.

Only a part of the plan can be expressed in the form of Product Backlog, and there is far more to it – UX research, studying new technology, expanding the team, deciding a pivot, stakeholder management, and so on. Make sure the whole plan is open and visible to all the team members. Involve them in planning so that everyone can think about the big picture.

Plan is not a splitted down future. Plan to make the future. You have a vision which dictates what you want to achieve in the future. It should include people benefited in some way, preferably through some functionality of your product. There's a huge gap between implementing a functionality and someone actually using it. Be strategic and come up with an ordered steps to realize that situation.

Early items might be about gathering information or testing hypotheses and they may not look like progress. But gaining knowledge IS progress. Planning to walk straight in the wilderness does not yield a feasible plan at all. You read maps, scout around, talk with someone familiar with the surroundings, and try to find the best way. Those are all necessities hence have value. When you're agile, new knowledge is your nourishment for survival.

As the product is getting formed, the backlog will mostly consist of adding or enhancing features. It's easy to think that the order is unimportant and the point is only when they will be released. As an agile coach Miho Nagase put it, all features yet to be realized are hypotheses and need to be tested by releasing it. You always have a chance to gain knowledge by doing tasks, especially releasing to the world, which should change the plan. Be rigorous in hunting for unknowns, especially when you feel you already know enough.

Care for the present. Don't get overwhelmed by the immediate.
You must survive and for that you need to focus on the present. Look for risks which might end your journey and gather information to evaluate the risks. Abilities and functionalities for analysis about your product are crucial so build them early. Team members and stakeholders are also important sources of information. A nice little trick is to ask everyone about the weather – do they think coming days will be sunny and joyful, a strong gust might hamper their progress, or perhaps someone senses a dark thunderous cloud on the horizon.

In one of my cases, it was a fatal mistake to misunderstand a sponsor who was kind and supportive and at the same time hard on business decisions. Clarify what someone can do to harm you (or aid you) and try to understand their own motives, success criteria, and responsibilities.

The present looks certain and you easily think of something important which must be done now. But the future being uncertain does not mean it's not important. Evaluate the future impact or outcome of tasks or items. What if it's not done now? What if it's done later? Or what if it's not done at all? An urgent item with smaller impact in the future must have lower priority than an lackluster item with larger impact in the future.

One interesting technique suggested by Yoh Nakamura is coloring items by their expected time of impact. For example, blue for functions released to users immediately, orange for internal stuff for long-term improvements, green for tasks to build a large enhancement which takes months to complete. Make sure the current or the next sprint is "colorful" enough through refinements. When you see only the short items in your backlog, it might indicate that you're overwhelmed by the immediate. Take some time to rebreathe and look into the future, together with the team, forcibly if need be.

A single path to reach the future
Imagine you need to boil two kinds of noodles in a pot. The short one takes 3 minutes to boil. The long one takes 10 minutes. I guess you start boiling the long one first, probably 7 minutes earlier than the short one. That's the way you plan. Then, imagine again, you also need to boil another noodle, the uncertain one, that you don't know how long it takes to boil. Which will you start boiling first, the long or the uncertain? Why?

It's not about a balance between the short and the long. It's about deciding what to do and when, considering when you want to deliver. You, as a team, are going to face an unending series of decisions and choices under complexity and uncertainty. There will be a path after where you tread, a single track of your steps. Actually the path is also laid toward the future reaching your vision, just you cannot see it. Your next step, in the short, must let you survive now and also it must depend a good deal on where you want to get to, in the long.

Of course short and long are relative. The coming sprint is nearer than the coming months. The coming month is nearer than the coming fiscal year. "The long" can be years or decades. When you plan for the future, remember that your decision will affect the future and everyone involved with its long tail which fades away in an ambiguous landscape in the

Through this work we have come to value

far.

Tsutomu Yasui

7. Individuals and interactions over processes and tools

7.1 The scrum police are coming for you (or are they?)

Over the past few years Scrum has moved away from being a loosely defined framework. PDFs like the Scrum Guide have codified much of Scrum. To some extent this has been useful. But it's also lead to the rise of the Scrum Police.

The Scrum Police are those who are quick to tell us any time we are doing something that isn't Scrum.

Have a ten-person team or a two-person team, be prepared for someone to tell you that isn't Scrum.

Dare to encourage your product owner to participate in daily scrums, be prepared for someone to tell you that isn't Scrum. Have one person be both Scrum Master and product owner, and you'll definitely hear that isn't Scrum.

And I want to tell you: I don't care.

And neither should you.

If someone tells you that what you're doing isn't Scrum, smile and walk away knowing that you might be doing something better than Scrum.

Sure: If you are new to Scrum, you almost certainly should do it by the book. But do it by any of the many good books on

Scrum. There are over a dozen, and they differ in details. And that's a good thing.

Follow a proven guide at first. Then as you get experience, experiment. Push the boundaries of Scrum. Try new things. Don't accept the dogma of any supposed Scrum Police, whether industry gurus or experts within your organization.

And then share your experience with those experiments–successful or not–with the rest of Scrum world. As the Agile Manifesto says, our goal should be "uncovering better ways of developing software by doing it and helping others do it."

Don't adhere unquestioningly to rules. The last thing an agile team should want is a framework whose "rules are immutable," as one popular online description of Scrum says. There are no Scrum police. The mere idea that there could be should be abhorrent to any team built on the ideas of inspect and adapt; that is, to any team that considers itself agile.

Ignoring the Scrum police and instead experimenting with promising variations of how your team works will allow you to succeed with agile.

Mike Cohn

7.2 Different Ideas for Defect Management

Frustration with the way in which defects are reported and managed may be due to a lack, or absence, of conversation. It seems that many testers adopt a bug tracking tool as the only way to communicate problems, with little consideration to establishing team relationships. Finding a bug is a perfect excuse for a tester to speak to a developer; utilise this opportunity!

Visual management board

I worked in a team with a visual management board that was frequently referred to and updated throughout the day, not just at our morning stand up meeting. Upon completing a task, both developers and testers would determine their next activity by visiting the board.

We used the same board for defect management. If issues were discovered during testing, I would write each one on a sticky note and attach it to the board. In this team, issues generally manifested in the user interface and were relatively simple to reproduce. A sticky note usually captured enough information for the problem to be understood by others.

New defects would be picked up as a priority when a developer visited the board in search of a new task. They would place their avatar on the defect, and then speak to me about anything that they didn't understand, or wanted to question the validity of. As problems were resolved, the developer would commit their change to the repository and we would swap my avatar onto the task. Bugs would then move to "done" in the same manner as other tasks on the board.

Desk delivery

In another team, there was a visual management board, but this would only reflect reality immediately after our daily stand up had occurred. Unlike the previous scenario, there was little point in sticking bugs on the board. It wasn't being used often enough. Instead I would take them directly to the developer who was working on the story.

My sticky note delivery style varied depending on the developer. One developer was quite happy for me to arrive at his desk, read out what was written on each note, then talk about the problems. Another preferred that I show her each defect in her local version of the application so that she was sure she understood what to change.

The developers would work from a set of sticky note defects lined up along their desk. As they resolved problems they would return the associated note to me. Having to transfer the physical object increased the opportunity for conversation and helped create relationships. There was also a healthy level of competition in trying not to have the most sticky notes stuck to your desk!

Cloud-based visual model

In a team without a constant physical board, I decided to communicate information about my testing using a cloud based visual model. I created a mind map to show my test ideas, reflect progress through testing, and to record defects, which were highlighted in red and had an attached note that explained the problem.

When I completed a testing task, I would send the developers a link via instant messaging to the cloud-based visual model. They could see where the problems were, and would respond with questions if anything was unclear. They seemed to like being able to see defects within a wider context, and were quite positive about a nifty new tool!

Bug tracking tool

Using a bug tracking tool may be essential to manage a high volume of problems with associated logs. However communicating via the tool alone is often ineffective. When I worked with a developer based in another country, he would arrive at work to an inbox full of notifications from the bug tracking system reflecting the problems resolved, remaining and discovered during our day. The volume of these messages meant that he occasionally missed information that was important, or prioritised his time incorrectly.

Katrina Clokie

7.3 Facilitate Learning

XKCD COMIC: HTTPS://XKCD.COM/1053/

Don't make fun of people admitting they don't know things...

This tip, in a nutshell, is "Facilitate learning."

You might think this is simple, but it isn't. There are many barriers. One significant problem is that, as in any industry where intelligence and knowledge are prized, if you look under the surface you will find that everybody is terrified of looking stupid.

To avoid looking stupid, people will do whatever they can to look clever. Sadly this means they may be reluctant to admit the gaps in their knowledge. Even more sadly, they may loudly judge others for *not being clever enough.* This in turn means that everybody is trying to avoid being judged in this way... which includes *hiding their knowledge gaps* and judging others as well.

It is therefore your job to do whatever you can to foster a culture of learning. A crucial part of this is encouraging people to be honest about what they need to learn in order to contribute effectively to your team. You can do this in the following ways:

1. Never judge anyone for their ignorance.
2. Lead by example: Confidently ask simple questions at every opportunity, and encourage others – particularly technical leaders – to do the same.
3. Encourage everybody to view knowledge gaps in a positive light: They should be an exciting opportunity to both teach and learn.
4. Foster a culture of learning. Celebrate learning. Instead of praising knowledge, praise the *thirst* for knowledge.
5. Remember that it is impossible to sustain a career as an IT professional unless you are prepared to keep learning. There is no professional in existence who does not have gaps in their knowledge. It is possible to have a long and successful career and still never learn, *or need to learn*, an area of knowledge which may seem crucial to somebody who has followed a slightly different career path. Therefore it is pointless to judge somebody for their knowledge gaps.

Clare Sudbery

7.4 Arrive with you whole heart

If you want individuals to be the best they can be, they need to be able to arrive at work with their whole selves (as opposed to their work selves). Many people have a different persona at work than to home. This takes a lot of concentration and creates stress. Its ok to be YOU at work. As a Scrum Master you need to encourage this and of course model the behaviour you would like your team to embrace.

If you had a bad nights sleep, let the team know. Allow them to help you.

If you're feeling great, and can take on more, help your team out.

Also take care of yourself. Forcing yourself to work an 8 hour day because its expected when you are not at your best, sends a message to your team that that behaviour is expected.

Talk to your team about arriving with your whole heart and what that means.

Actively and continuously open your heart to your team.

Samantha Laing & Karen Greaves

7.5 Care about feedback

There are many kinds of feedback for an Agile team to look for and to benefit from to deliver impactful product together. My tip is about what happens between human beings, when feedback is given/received. I want to share a personal story, and the tools and practices that inspire me and I use the most (whether in an Scrum Master position or not!).

"One deserves to know"
I once had a conversation with a team member that I found quite unpleasant and left me hurt, feeling misunderstood and not valued. When rehashing it with a friend, my friend asked me if I thought that the team member was aware of what didn't feel right for me during the conversation. What clicked

for me is when she said "Don't you think she deserves to know?". That got me thinking indeed... My train of thoughts was something like this: I am the team's Scrum Master. I value feedback and human interactions. If the situation was reversed, would I want to know?

Curious alignment of stars, at that time, I stumbled upon a talk from Kim Scott about Radical Candor[1]. To me, not giving feedback to this team member about how our conversation made me feel, and not trying to understand what happened so that we could avoid it to repeat in the future, was a little bit like not telling someone she has a chunk of salad stuck in her teeth...

So, I had another conversation with that team member, where I simply told her about how I felt, giving specific examples, and tried to learn more about her side of the conversation.

Empathy and introspection

I tried to empathise with my team member, to understand (all assumptions and guesses before I met with her a second time) what was going on on her side, and what values or beliefs of her I might have hurt myself.

I also examined my own feelings. A friend-coach (thank you Thierry Conter) had told me "Behind every 'no', there is a 'yes, if...'", and I sought to understand what could have been different in that conversation that would have made it ok for me.

Thinking in details about what I felt made it easier to use Non-Violent Communication (NVC) during our 2nd conversation. I recalled specific facts or sentences, explained how I felt and why (what need of mine wasn't fulfilled) and when I could, ended with a request/description of a change that I wished for. "Focusing on me" can seem like a selfish/egocentric

---

[1]https://www.radicalcandor.com/about-radical-candor/

way of having a conversation, and NVC feels awkward the first times. I find it very powerful, and also liberating. In French, Jacques Salomé calls the opposite the "Klaxon communication": because "you" translate to "tu" in French, and a conversation where the sentences start with "tu ... tu ... tu ..." really sounds like a unpleasant noisy place (I guess in English "you..you...you..." would be "hooter communication"?).

Relationship scarf

Also, a conversation has two participants, and one only owns one's side of an exchange (the metaphor Salomé uses is the "relationship scarf"): expressing my own feelings and using "I" helps with that responsibility and ownership. To me, that's a helpful technique to give feedback respectfully.

Another tool that I find extremely useful and powerful to provide feedback in a respectful and meaningful way is the Perfection game[2] (from the Core Protocols[3]). This protocol requires the feedback giver to list things that she liked about the thing, and suggest concrete improvements that would make the think perfect. I've found this format invites more positivity and kindness, and is actionable.

With that tool like with any other, what the receiver does with the feedback is her own responsibility.

Receiving feedback

When I am in the 'receiver' position, I try to remember to choose only between two reactions:

- Say "thank you". Actually, I believe we should always thank the feedback giver, even when the feedback didn't feel wrapped in empathy and kindness or even felt like blame. One can still be thankful for being given the opportunity to learn about the consequences of her actions!

---

[2]http://www.hanoulle.be/2010/07/perfection-game/
[3]https://liveingreatness.com/core-protocols/

- Ask for more: "Can you say more/provide more details, maybe describing a situation when that happened?"
What I try to avoid is to react against it, rush and try to explain myself, or even deny it. Although I think trying to understand (and help the other understand) the context and what caused the behaviour can be useful, I think that shouldn't be the first reaction to feedback. The bare minimum is to show you've listened to your interlocutor and understood her intention and what she meant.

Care about feedback, treat it as a gift: give it with kindness, receive it with openness

Emilie Franchomme

7.6 Build your network

When you first start with agile, you are mostly working within your team. That's fine! There are a lot of important improvements that happen within the team. Eventually though you'll hit into some organisational impediments and you will need assistance from people outside your team.

Individuals and interactions over processes and tools - that's not just for building software but for everything you need to get done in an organisation.

The team wants to convert a conference room into a team room? Your team wants budget to buy a dedicated build server? Your chances are much brighter if the decision makers already know you, trust you and believe in you.

Participate in company events and volunteer in committees where you can meet and work with these people in other contexts. Building trust takes a lot of time, so start getting to know the rest of your organisation from day one.

Siddharta Govindaraj

7.7 Processes should enhance people's ability to work, not prevent it.

At various jobs, I've been responsible for creating processes for agile engineering teams. One thing I've often seen is a misunderstanding of the tenet "Individuals and interactions over processes and tools". That quote gets used as an argument against the effort of creating and trying out new processes, and I think it can be better clarified as "Processes that support the people". Without a shared process, there's a higher tendency to silo, or confusion around who's responsible for what. Having clear processes are useful - but they need to be flexible enough to iterate without breaking. Processes should enhance people's ability to work, not prevent it.

Angela Riggs

7.8 Happy Storming

In order for a group of people to form into a team, they will need to learn how to fight with each other about issues that matter to them. From the very start encourage them to talk to each other and provoke discussions that are contentious rather than avoid them. An ability to argue constructively about big issues comes from practice, practice that is gained arguing about small issues.

A technique I've learned recently is to ask the team to raise any blockers or things that the whole team should know. Once they have spoken, they nominate the next person to speak. As a scrum master I pay attention to who they nominate. Is it always the same person or do they seem cautious when they nominate them. This helps you see the dynamics in the team.

Chris Matts

7.9 Crafting quality interactions

One of the big lessons I keep learning is that the quality of the output of any given group or team is directly proportional to the quality of the interactions between that group. Setting yourselves up for exceptional interactions can make all the difference.

I was coaching a few coaches at a large organisation. All three were fabulous in their way, and all three were quite different. One day during a role-play session, Steve became frustrated with Claire. The two had had some underlying tension that had been building and no mechanisms to speak about it. Their mentals models of the world were also very different, and sometimes they weren't able to see each other's point of view. On this particular day, Steve left the room quite vocal in his frustration. I realised we needed to discuss what had happened so that we could all move forward constructively.

When Steve got back, I asked if we could have a conversation about what had happened. All the coaches agreed. The first thing we did was create what I called an Alliance, specifically for the interaction that was about to take place. What did we want to have as the ground rules, and what did we want to keep front of mind. I can't remember everything that was on the alliance, but I remember that respect and listening to understand were there.

It had a noticeable impact on the conversation. I also observed that it had an impact on me because it was front of mind. We made it physical and visible on a flip chart.

I start all my training with a Training Alliance, my team has a Team Alliance, and any new team I coach, one of the first things that I do is facilitate an Alliance for the team. It doesn't matter what you call it what matters is that you have something. You can call it an Alliance, a Team Agreement, Rules of engagement, anything. Start somewhere and start talking about what is essential for everyone in your interactions. Write it down and make it visible. Take it into all events, and make it new when you have new people. Make it a living document and review it regularly.

It has helped me and my team and the teams that I have worked with, and I am sure it can help you too.

Joanne Perold

7.10 9 Rules of thumb to improve your backlog refinement workshops

1. Do it more often – try twice a week

Plan to workshop stories or do backlog refinement multiple times a week. It'll make the sessions quicker. And, if questions come up that the group can't answer, you can do some research and bring the story back later in the week.

2. Make attendance non-mandatory

When people are forced to attend a workshop they're often unengaged. If they're not engaged, you won't have a good discussion, and leave with the shared understanding you need. Ironically, including everyone with the hope that they all leave with shared understanding can result in no one leaving with shared understanding.
As long as you have a small balanced group that includes someone who understands the
functionality, someone who can build it, and someone who can test it, you'll have a good
discussion. Let groups know ahead of time what you'll be talking about, and allow them to opt in, or leave if they're not interested or engaged. If someone who wasn't there needs details later, they need only talk with a team member who was there.

3. Keep the working group small

Groups of 2-5 can have an effective conversation. If you more want to participate, try a fish-bowl facilitation approach.

4. Don't project your backlog tool on the wall – use the whiteboard

Everyone can engage sketch their ideas on the whiteboard. Everyone can add their own sticky notes with ideas. Use tools that allow everyone to discuss, visualize ideas, and engage.

Even when working remotely, try to use tools, like google docs, that allow participants on all sides to make changes to a virtual document.

5. Don't start with acceptance criteria, take time to discuss and visualize how the functionality might look and work first.

It's just hard to arrive at good acceptance criteria if everyone doesn't have the same
understanding of how the software should work. Take time to make sure you're in agreement
about how it works first.

6. Use acceptance criteria to confirm you have shared understanding

After you're reasonably confident the team has the same idea in mind about what they're
building, discuss how you'll confirm you've built the right thing. It's OK if this discussion results in a bit of back-tracking. That's why you're having it.

Acceptance criteria, or the "confirmation" part of the story, is our agreement on what it means to be done with the story. I like using these questions to drive out acceptance criteria:

1. What will we check to confirm this story is done?
2. How will we demonstrate this story at sprint review?
3. How will we measure success when this feature or capability is released?

7. Do talk about technical details

It's OK for developers to discuss how they'd implement it and consider options. Because, if it's expensive to build, we may want to consider alternative designs. Or, not build it at all.

8. Do estimate

Discussing how complex it would be to build will help confirm you have shared understanding about how it works. It might force discussions of technical trade-offs. And it may change what you choose to build.

9. Do split stories into the smallest testable parts possible

Don't expect stories to come into the workshop "right-sized" for development. This is what the workshop is for. Use the deeper understanding you've built during the workshop to break the story down into the smallest buildable and testable parts you can.

Jeff Patton

7.11 Ownership in Agile: Purpose and collaboration

We live in a world that still thinks that "silos mean simple". This is an entrenched belief, and it's not simple to act against it, even if, intellectually we do agree that our capability to adapt depends on the quality of our collaboration.
While working with teams, I realised that holding roles is a siloting trap.
My tip from the trenches of Agile and systemic coaching is a

distributed ownership of what each
role holds.

Product Ownership and the meaning of life

My first example is the Product Owner, a very hard role to
have. While the Product Owner needs to be 100% available
to the team to answer questions and give feed-back, she
also needs to build strategic and facilitate groups of business
stakeholders. And of course, write and validate the backlog,
etc. In earlier days, I have come across development teams
angry of their not enough available, not enough User Stories
skilled product owners. This dynamic is disempowering both
sides. I believe true value and move forward dynamics lies in
a shared ownership.

What is the shared ownership? First of all, recognise that
everyone involved in a project has a stake. If that is true,
take the time to acknowledge the shared dream with all
stakeholders.

My first question when I arrive to work with a team is what
is your shared dream? What do you thing that, by working
together, will improve the life of customers and how does that
relates with your own narrative.

Some people might tell that is is too idealistic. This reminds
me a quote of Satish Kumar who says "People tell me I'm
not realistic enough, I'm an idealist. Then I answer , well the
wold has been led by realistic people, do you like the result?"
I believe true ownership comes through what really moves
you through life. Otherwise it's bureaucracy. For this reason,
while I do recognise the importance of the Product Owner's
role, product ownership is a mindset that all stakeholders can
have.

My tip to work out your product ownership mindset :
For any action and decision, answer the question : What is
my contribution so this product is making the life better for
its users?

Own the team you're part of

My second example is the Scrum Master role. I perceive it like
another try of our simplification biases to silos the roles. I have
come across teams where the was a lot of confusion around
who should hold the role of Scrum Master. In some teams,
there was an attempt to translate the manager role into that
of a Scrum Master. Big confusion unfolds, as the manager just
does not know anymore what her posture should be. Another
pattern I have seen is external consultancy Scrum Masters.
While this second option can work , I have a preference for
another set up: Invite the team to own the Scrum Master role
by themselves. If I step in a team as an Agile coach, this is one
of the first set-up I suggest.

We cannot push new ways of working onto people. The only
condition people will adopt new ways of working is to be
willing to do so. The only way they will adopt those new
ways is by experimenting them in their own reality. Fo this
reason, I propose the role of Scrum Master to someone who
is part of the team, usually the person that has most affinity
with facilitation and is the most enthusiast about Agile Teams
dynamics. You may call her the "early adopter".

Unlike a set up where the Scrum Master is an external expert
that downloads her expertise onto the team, having the Scrum
Master as a member of the team, makes change more organic.
Transformation comes from within the team, as the Scrum
Master being part of the team, knows well the operational
reality of that team. An Agile Coach who supports both the

Scrum Master and the team can be an external expert. This is the way I work with teams.

Over time, when teams gain experience with Agile, I have seen the role of the Scrum Master evolving to either to become a shifting role - everyone on the team takes the role for a given period of time like 2 sprints, or even more extreme, when teams feel mature enough they don't need a Scrum Master anymore, they are living by Agile principles and practices. They have Agile Ownership.

My ultimate tip : The key of change is ownership. Own the purpose of what you do along with your team, organisation, business, community... Own the interactions you want to have with your pairs and all other stakeholders.

Oana Juncu

7.12 The gut feeling ordering practice

Having started my professional career as employee number 12 taught me a lot about entrepreneurship, having an engaging purpose and lot's of freedom to do what is necessary to get things done. I especially liked the camaraderie and simplicity of the structures we worked in which I valued when being absorbed into a 15k+ organisation.

Today (May2020), 20+ years after the start of my career I still value camaraderie and simplicity. It drives me to address specific pain points in the system which prevent me from feeling its power again. For example:
+ Horizontal complexity- consolidating functions across the enterprise

+ Vertical complexity - shedding obsolete roles, layers and reporting structures
+ Spatial complexity - preparing distributed / remote teams for success

One of the key factors that drives a turn-around in strong beliefs within organisations is having a single Product Backlog for very large products where 100's, 1000's of people are contributing to it. An overall Product Backlog as recommended by LeSS (Large-Scale Scrum). I've been part of introducing this concept in many different organisations, many different markets and I keep being astonished about the urge to avoid collaboration and put things in processes and tools.

I always recommend people to rely on data analytics (user engagement data, market analysis, competitor analysis...); collaboration across many departments, customers, partners... and rely on a gut feeling that arises from that work to order the single Product Backlog and drive their business. Close to every time my recommendations are being ignored and people come with the idea to delegate the ordering of backlog items to one or another formula. Like there is a magic formula to create an amazing business?!

At first the formula seems to be relatively simple but soon they discover that it is missing some part. Why? Their gut is telling them ⊠. What happens next? Another factor is added to the formula and everybody is happy again, no discussions, collaboration needed to order the Product Backlog. And this scenario repeats itself many times till the formula becomes that complex that only a mathematical wizz kid can make sense out of it.

A couple of months, sometimes more than a year later the formula is ditched in favor of collaboration and guts with access to good data that ensures empirically-sound decision making. As a result, the system becomes leaner, more customer-centric and ready with each successive change wave to build its greatest products yet.

The astonishment I have is that this seems to happen many times even though I can bring many stories and examples. Changing mindsets, adjusting strong beliefs and enabling true collaboration seems to be harder than I assume it to be and the above pattern is inevitable. Be patient!

Jürgen De Smet

7.13 Creating Collaborative Connective tissues

What I often find is that coaches, leaders and organisations focus on the processes and tools of agile methods, believing that they will deliver the collaboration, trust and culture change that true agility achieves.

My advice always when asked to help is, let's think about what you're really trying to achieve, never forget what lies at the heart of agility is creating information flow both horizontally and vertically through the organisation in order to enable the directional decisions that allow us to inspect, adapt and ultimately deliver.

Information flow being anything that enables you to make directional decisions that decide the direction of travel dependent on your role. Examples of this could be risks, dependencies, a more efficient way of writing the code, impediments, progress metrics.

So having said that, we should think about how you might create and enable those collaborative connective tissues that allow the information to flow both horizontally and vertically through the teams and ultimately the organisation.

Whatever tools, processes and structures you are about to put in place ask yourself:

- Will they make collaboration better?
- Will they radiate information from the organisation to every level of the organisation?
- Will they create information flow that enables expedient fact based directional decisions rather than opinion based decisions?

When you do this the connective collaborative tissues of the organisation come alive and are permeated by a culture of trust and transparency.

Last of all, contribute personally to creating those collaborative connective tissues by improving the quality of yours and the organisations listening. As my friend and mentor Alistair Cockburn often says when asked how to improve collaboration, "Listen with generosity, curiosity and wonder"

Tony Ponton

7.14 Self-Organized teams

"Self-Organized teams" are an essential ingredient of Agile. It is one of the key traits that make product development a successful course. If you are wondering what a Self-Organized team looks like and the expectations from such a team, then this post might sound interesting to you!

Self-Organization has its origins spotted from nature including animals, birds, science, and humans. It can be defined as the collective behavior of living species; it is a state of mind where the species within the group synchronize their behavior in response to the environmental trigger to achieve the best outcome! This behavior emerges organically without any instructions being given to the group.

Self-organizing systems can be found all around us that include cells in our bodies, bird flocks, fish pools, and ant colonies. Studies indicated that self-organizing systems need the required support from the environment for them to co-exist and function, and most importantly the individual species in such groups are driven by a common mindset and behavioral instincts.

For example, fishes in schools use their visual abilities and lateral lines to organize themselves based on some fixed set of rules. Every fish follows these rules and the collaborative effort of all those leads to self-organizing behavior.

Self-Organized group effectiveness depends on the collective behavior of everyone in the group. The environment should be supportive of providing such groups with the right stimuli for example in case of a fish pool, the stimuli provided by the environment is in the form of food and water to survive.

Thus for self-organizing teams to emerge and sustain, there needs to be –

- A supportive environment
- A basic set of rules to drive consistent behavior
- Everyone in the group responding collaboratively to the triggers
- The self-organizing team is

- responsible for its own success;
- make its own decisions, decide the best course of action, of course within the boundaries of the operating container.

This is the same for humans as well, for such teams to foster, they need a container with some basic essentials provided within which they can thrive learn and respond to the external stimuli like meeting the goals, deciding their course of action, or protecting themselves from external threats.

Madhavi Ledalla

8. Working software over comprehensive documentation

8.1 Manage the shape of your backlog.

Think of it as the rocks that go into an ore crusher when mining for diamonds. Big chunks go into the top, most of which gets discarded as the rocks are broken down into smaller and smaller pieces, leaving just the valuable gems to be implemented by the team.

Explanation:

The backlog is a prioritised list of things that need to be done in order build a product which makes customers happy. The most common approach to building this backlog today is to use User Stories, often in the format "as a <role> I want <feature or capability> so that <element of value can be achieved>. The most frequent mistake that product owners and teams make is to produce a lengthy laundry list of user stories. Resist that temptation and think of the backlog as an ore-crusher. Large chunky stories (call them epics and features if you want, they're just big stories) should be at the top of the funnel and as the team works through delivering value and getting feedback they progressively break them down into smaller and smaller pieces, discarding most of what we thought we wanted and exposing the real gemstones which are the stories that truly contribute to the value in the product.

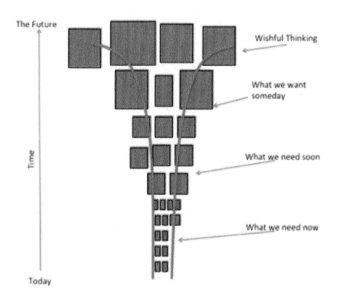

The shape of a healthy backlog

The stories that come out of the bottom of the backlog are small enough for the team to deliver using their agile development practices. Ideally, they should be fully implementable (per the agreed-upon definition of done) in half an iteration or less — the smaller our stories, the better our ability to predict and plan work. However, for those stories that are far away, we want to keep the level of detail coarse. The reality is that our understanding of what is needed will evolve significantly based on what happens as the product is delivered, and much of what we currently understand will turn out to be mistaken or obsolete.

Shane Hastie

8.2 Build Systems, not Software

80% of what you need to do to manage your team's work can be accomplished with index cards on a wall. Of the part that remains, 80% can be managed with a spreadsheet. Of the part that remains, 80% can be done with simple CRUD programs. Why must it be different for your customers? Systems engineering means understanding the customer's problem within the customer's own environment. You can't take their word for it. You must see for yourself.

Some software absolutely must be written. Nobody wants to play a video game or drive an automobile that involves handling index cards. But a great deal of software is created that never should be made. Don't jump into technological solutions just because your team title says Development. All new technology is technical debt. Some of it just has better financial returns that justify the investment. You do your team more favors by insisting that sufficient analysis and design has been done to demonstrate that new software is necessary.

So, don't deliver Working Software. Deliver Working Systems and try to do it with as little software as possible.

Corey Ladas

8.3 Every team needs a Working Agreement

Do you have a working agreement in your team?

Unless your team is highly skilled at mindreading and doesn't ever make any assumptions, you may want to consider creating one!

Working agreement (aka Team Norms) – is a short list of behaviours or actions that a team agrees to engage in (and hold themselves accountable to) on a regular basis. One of the really cool things about Working Agreements – they are created by the team! And they get created in the language and the choice of word of the team.

One of my favourite working agreements story is from a team of interns I worked with over the summer. Their Team Norms included a statement like

"One diva, one mic".

This was their unique and beautiful way to express:

"Take turns, when speaking. Be respectful, listen, don't interrupt."

As a Scrum Master you can certainly help to facilitate the process, offer techniques to engage everyone's voice, but you can't create their Working Agreements on behalf of your team! It is for them to bring out what's the most important.

Why does a team need working agreements?

1. To clarify assumptions about what's acceptable in this team.
2. To acknowledge and embrace the differences. (Hey, not everyone is a morning person!)
3. To help them stay as a team when things "go south".

How do you create working agreements?

There are many ways to do it.

It could be as simple as starting with a silent brainstorming, followed by affinity mapping and dot-voting to help select the top 5 – 7 ideas.

I like to add a bit more fun and a personal touch to this by asking team members to pair up and interview each other, using modified personal maps[1]. For the personal map questions, I mix in a few about family, hobbies, favourite vacation spots with the ones that lead to the working agreements conversation:

- I work best when...
- One this team I'd like to learn...
- Something that can really trigger me is...
- Top 3 things you can expect from me are...

I also ask each pair to come up with one answer that is an "exaggerated truth". After about 6 minutes, team members take turns and introduce their pair to the rest of the team (using the personal maps they created in their interviews).

This is when the team gets to learn about everyone, laugh, while trying to guess the exaggerated answer...

And this is when a facilitator gets to capture highlights of these introductions in "Same/Different" poster. These highlights become the basis for narrowing down on the Working Agreements choices for this team. (and some team members get to find their new skiing buddies too!)

Are Working Agreements carved in stone?

Of course not!

You can help the team and keep them alive by reviewing them in your retrospectives. Why not facilitate a self-assessment on Working agreements? Ask your team next time:

"How are we holding ourselves to our team norms? Are they still relevant?"

---

[1]https://management30.com/practice/personal-maps/

Another opportunity to bring them up, when you have a team composition change: a new team member joining or someone leaving the team.

Last but definitely not least, team working agreements will help your team to stay civil during a conflict. Refer to them when things get heated. Then discuss with the team what needs to be added to the Working Agreements to navigate conflict more effectively next time.

What are you waiting for? Go ahead, give it a try. Experiment with Working Agreements in your team and have fun doing it!

Dana Pylayeva

8.4 Effective Teams are NOT Efficient

Your favourite football team is playing a game. The goalkeeper rarely has a need to move, let alone touch the ball - the rest of the team plays in the other half of the field. Players are calm, focused, and while the opposing players run like crazy to then just miss the ball ... our players just seem to be where they need to be when they need to be there... without much visible movement or effort.

That's an effective team. Obviously, we won.

Imagine another football team. Everyone seems keen to make an effort. They run, they sweat, they swear. Sometimes, they get the ball, and they surely move it around a lot. You think they'd be a lot happier if everyone had a ball, that would keep them even busier - and maybe happier. Everyone in that team is delivering a lot of work, putting a lot of effort in, creating a lot of "output", during the 90 minutes. The players are well trained, they look great, they move fast... They are very efficient runners. They are very efficient ball movers (if they get it - hence your thought about giving them more balls). They lose.

This is an ineffective team.

Effective teams are not efficient. Or, more precisely, effective teams don't make efficient use of their players.

Effective teams make sure that the work moves fast. Not the workers.

What is the difference?

Your car can go very efficiently in the wrong direction, and that is not effective. A single thing like a car can be efficient and effective - especially when it is a highly predictable machine - an organic entity with multiple independent agents can't. Or, to be more precise: you can't make efficient use of all parts when you want the whole to be effective. The parts need to be available to help each other.

Imagine your favourite orchestra, jazz or rock band. Some of the most beautiful, touching, sensational moments of music involve very few players, are solos or duets - when most of the players are not playing. Are they still being paid? Would you want them to leave the stage and join another band for the time their piece gives them a break?

That depends on how predictable your game, your work, your kind of music, is.

In a classical orchestra, playing a classical symphony, when the drummer is only needed in the fourth movement (classical music doesn't have a lot of drums, in case you did not notice), then - theoretically - he could join the stage after movement number three. He could do some other work somewhere else in the meantime, which would be a more efficient use of his time. Most conductors and orchestra leaders I know would still prefer them to be there, on stage - because they are part of the team. And the team shows up together to do the work.

In more flexible, improvised, spontaneous kinds of bands - think jazz - it's fairly unthinkable that someone is part of the band and not with the band. (Obviously, as we are talking about art, even the unthinkable is quite possible ...) The score is not decided in advance so everyone has to be there to create it together. A lot of work in today's organisations is like that. We have goals and strategy and purpose, but not necessarily a detailed plan. Teams figure out what to do while they work - and that's great, that's where creativity and innovation come from.

And that is not efficient. It does not need to be.

In fact, focusing on efficiency will kill effective creation of value.

Why does this matter?

Many organisations in today's less predictable world want to be "more agile". They are looking for resilience, innovation, speed of response. They want to foster creativity and collaboration. And the are asking coaches and Scrum Masters to help them get there.

Leaders and managers in many of those organisations are used to managing the capacity of their people in a simple way: they optimise for 100% "resource utilisation". I'm putting the term in quotation marks because I don't particularly like to call people resources. There must be some management school somewhere that teaches this principle. It works well for very few problems, not even for machines: assume your car was constructed with the intention of using all the gearwheels (or any other parts) equally all the time - wouldn't that be a nightmare?

The effectiveness of most systems depends on the inefficient use of its parts. The less predictable and regular the internal operation of the system is, the more this is the case.

If efficiency (efficient use of resources/parts/team members) had a place in a team ...

- Football teams would play with eleven balls
- In a good football game (when the whole rest of the team is in the other half of the field) the goalkeeper would keep another team's goal instead
- Musicians would always all play at the same time
- Team members would spend more time doing their own work instead of working with each other.
- Team members would frequently be exhausted, feel overworked, and left alone with "my problem".

Really effective teams

- Play with only one ball at a time
- Solve one problem, run one experiment or implement one feature at a time
- Have slack, so that they are ready to deal with surprises
- Are relaxed so that they can regularly step back and understand the whole
- Are confident enough to not get rushed and busy.
- Have enough freedom to be engaged, learn, improve and have fun. That's another factor (which is probably not true for the parts of a machine) that makes them do better work, faster.

Availability

I remember a key conversation with the head of a 1000 people IT support organisation many years ago, about the configuration of a new capacity planning system. To make an informed suggestion, I asked what he wanted to achieve with the system. He replied, "my job is to make sure that all of my people are 100% planned in projects." I paused a moment and asked, "let me rephrase... you are leading an IT service organisation for thousands of users. And your primary goal in your capacity planning is that when any one of those users calls you, no one will be available to take the call?"

Practical

So, what does a Scrum Master do to support effectiveness rather than efficiency?

- Foster collaboration. Challenge people's assumptions about working together, and understand their fears (having somebody watch me work all day is scary).
- Pair with each and everyone on your team, again and again. Inspire them to do the same.
- Try Mob programming. It's even less efficient than pairing and often even more effective for the team. It's like playing football with only one ball in the game.

Olaf Lewitz

8.5 Empower "Team Change"

Many agile teams get together on a regular cadence to reflect on the work they are doing and how they are working together. This is typically called a retrospective. At companies that are growing fast and hiring a lot of team members, I also encourage these teams to reflect on their own team composition. How has their team changed in the past few months? What has this been like? What changes in their team composition would they like to see going forward? Do they feel they need to grow in size? Do they feel like they need to shift their team composition in different way?

I was with a team once, for example, that grew quite large and decided in a retrospective that they wanted to split in half in order to better focus their work. There were more than 13 people on this cross-functional team. In their retrospectives they talked about how standup meetings were taking longer - and planning meetings were even worse. What had typically taken an hour, now was more than two, and many people felt like they were wasting time because the work had diverged. One team member said, "Why should I listen to what they are doing, I'm never going to work on that." The idea of splitting the team in half came up. The engineers thought that in order to be more effective as a team, splitting into two teams would be helpful. The rest of the team, after analyzing and discussing this situation agreed.

The team wanted to move forward with splitting in half. They came up with a plan and brought it to their managers. They shared how they would divide up the codebase and how they would divide up the work. They worked out a new seating plan, and identified which technical tools needed to be updated with their team split - they made a new channel in their chat tool. They made a new email list. They scheduled a date on the calendar for when the "official team split" would happen. They had a "change desks" party where they played music, moved their stuff to a new desk, and ate pizza together. They named their new teams and working with their coach came up with team agreements. They owned their team change.

I've seen teams grow and split like this time and time again. It's a Dynamic Reteaming pattern - especially at companies where you are adding a lot of people and are doubling in size. Give teams the power to change their team's composition. Encourage that teams talk about their own composition within retrospective meetings. The people will have insight and tactical knowledge for how best to approach the work. Trust them. Empower your teams to organically shift your organisation.

Heidi Helfand

8.6 Study how the work works

When a team is not performing as expected, where does one look for problems? Yes..., the first thought is to look for causes in the team itself or its close surroundings. One tends to look for events that happened with the team not so long ago. Is it lousy team dynamics? Were the requirements misunderstood? Were people sick? Etc.

A quick fix is to assign a coach to work with the team and look for local solutions. It is easy for a coach to walk into the team room, attend some team meetings, do some interviews, review some code, and analyze some team dynamics. Then write a report for management, and give some suggestions for improvements before moving on to the next team.
But is the problem contextual to the team? Or is there a more systemic problem? And do the teams want coaching?

My tip is to start engagements with a Go See sessions to observe, ask questions, and show respect to the teams and leadership. Use the sessions to understand how the work is working for them at the level of a larger group. One essential thing I look for is recurring events that happen over weeks, patterns that keep coming back over time. Why? Because patterns are often the result of the organisational structure, processes, and policies. And these systemic issues can likely only be addressed by improving organizational design. Contrary to common belief, you cannot make a substantial improvement in systemic matters by working exclusively on the teams.

Rely on stories from people who work there, on personal observations, and humble inquiry to get insights into the system dynamics. With all this information, create an understanding of how the work works over time. Then use that systemic understanding to make transparent to the teams and leadership what could be going on. With these insights, the teams and the leaders come up with their suggestions for improvements.

Cesario Ramos

8.7 Working software over .... almost everything

Of course I agree with every line of the Agile Manifesto: as one of its authors, how could it be otherwise? But I do have a personal favorite:

Working software over comprehensive documentation.

My concern isn't documentation, comprehensive or otherwise: it's the absence of working software that bothers me. As I look back over my long history in software, it seems to me that most of the situations I encountered could have been much improved by having a working product ready to go, containing all the features that were finished at that time.

With that product on the table between us, my conversations with management and with sales could have moved to much more concrete decisions about what to do next. There might still have been great pressure to deliver, but with real software, ready to go, I could have guided the team to better conclusions. Or so it seems to me.

So, for me, if I were to give my past self any advice, and if I were to give today's developers any advice, my first suggestion would be "Always have a working software increment available."

Ron Jeffries

8.8 Technical Debt And Product Success

Similar to a company experiencing financial debt, products can incur "technical debt": This happens when wrong or suboptimal architecture, technology, and coding decisions are taken. Consequently, the architecture may not be as loosely coupled as it should be, and the code may be messy rather than clean. This article explains why product people should care about technical debt and it offers strategies for addressing it.

Why Technical Debt Matters for Product People

As the person in charge of the product, you may not be terribly concerned about how clean and well-structured the code is. But the quality of your product matters: It directly impacts your ability to achieve strategic product goals and make your products successful: Technical debt makes it hard to experiment with new ideas, release new features, and quickly respond to user feedback. [1]

The messier the code and the less modular the architecture is, the longer it takes and the more expensive it is to change your product. In the worst case, you have to go through a rewriting exercise where some parts or even the entire product are being redeveloped. This is similar to financial debt: When the debt is not paid back, the interest payments can multiply and eventually cripple the business.

Technical Debt and Your Product

To understand if and to what extent your product is affected by technical debt, talk to the development team, for example, in the next sprint retrospective. I find that development team members usually have a good understanding where issues in the architecture and code are.

Additionally, consider asking the team to collect data that shows how much technical debt there is, where it is located, and how bad it is, for example, by using code complexity, dependencies, duplication, and test coverage as indicators. There are a number of code analysis tools available that collect the appropriate data and show how adaptable the architecture and how clean the code is. [2]

Once you understand the amount and severity of tech debt in your product, analyse its impact on meeting the product goals and achieving product success together with the development team. Take into account the cost of delay, the cost of not addressing the technical debt now but delaying it to a future point in time. Should you, for example, continue adding new features to the product for the next six months and plan in bigger technical improvement work afterwards? Or would it be better to address the worst debt now?

Furthermore, consider the life cycle stage of your product. Technical debt is particularly bad for new and young products: If your product has a closely-coupled architecture with lots of dependencies, if it lacks (automated) tests and documentation, or if it is full of spaghetti code, then experimenting with new ideas and adapting the product to user feedback and new trends will be difficult and time-consuming. Similarly, if you want to extend its product life cycle, you may have to first remove (some of) the technical debt before you can make the necessary changes and add new features or create a variant.

Having said that, it is a valid strategy to launch a minimum viable product (MVP) whose architecture, technology, and code has been intentionally compromised in order to reduce time to market—as long as the quality is good enough to adapt the product to feedback from the early market. But apply this strategy with caution: You will have to spend time addressing the technical debt incurred and putting your product on solid technical foundations. This should be done before reaching product-market fit, as you will otherwise struggle to scale up and keep your product growing.

If, however, your product is in maturity—or even decline—and you do not intend to extend its life cycle but focus on maximising the business benefits it generates, you probably want to carry out as little debt removal work as possible.

Options for Removing Technical Debt

Once you've established how much tech debt there is and how soon it needs to be addressed, you face two choices: You can either make time for a focused effort and dedicate a period of time to removing the debt, or you can carry out the work in parallel to enhancing your product and adding new functionality.

Whenever you face a significant amount of tech debt that constitutes a barrier to innovation, you should opt for a dedicated period to remove it. Apple did this with Mac OS X Snow Leopard, which was released in 2009 after nearly two years of work. While Snow Leopard didn't provide any new functionality, it created the foundation for future releases by improving performance and reducing the memory footprint of the operating system, for example.

I am not suggesting that you should necessarily spend a year or more refactoring your product, as Apple did. But it can be more effective to make a concentrated effort and invest a few months, or at least a sprint or two, in cleaning up the software, as opposed to doing it in drips and drops across several releases. You intentionally slow down, so to speak, to go faster afterwards.

If a refactoring release is the right approach for you, then your product roadmap should reflect this: It should show a release dedicated to future-proofing the product and making the necessary technical changes.

But if the technical debt is not as significant and does not need to be addressed as urgently, then plan in time for removing some debt in every sprint while continuing to improve the user experience and add or enhance features. You can do this by adding tech debt remedial items to the product backlog. This makes the necessary work visible and allows you to track it across sprints and releases. Make sure, though, that the necessary work is actually carried out and requests for more functionality don't prevent the removal of technical debt. (My article "Succeeding with Innovation and Maintenance" discusses how you can fix bugs and add new features at the same time.)

Preventing Technical Debt

Intentionally compromising the code quality to get a release out and accepting technical debt is all good and well as long as you actually remove the debt afterwards. Often, however, technical debt is created unintentionally in my experience.

Digital products require ongoing attention to their architecture and code. Otherwise, the product quality will deteriorate, which leads to an increase in technical debt. This is very much like maintaining your bicycle on a regular basis, ideally after every ride. And the more you rely on your bike, the more you should care about it, clean it, and fix or replace faulty parts. The challenge is to make time for the necessary clean-up and maintenance work and view it as part of the bike riding experience, rather than a chore.

The same is true for digital products: Some teams feel so rushed and pressured that they repeatedly cut corners and don't apply good software craftsmanship practices like evolutionary architecture, test-driven development, pair programming, and continuous integration. But these practices do not only help create an adaptable architecture and clean code base. Used properly, they will **speed up** development and allow you to release new features and functionality **faster**, not slower—the latter being a common misconception amongst product people in my experience. The opposite is also true: If development teams don't apply the right practices and tools, then the software is likely to be brittle, not soft and malleable.

If you want to prevent future technical debt, then give your development team the time to learn, apply, and improve the right development practices. In fact, you should expect that the development team creates product increments with the right quality. A great way to do this is to employ a Definition of Done that states code complexity limits and test coverage targets, and to only accept work results that fulfil this definition.

Notes

[1] Technical debt is a concept originally suggested by Ward Cunningham[2] and nicely explained by Martin Fowler[3].

[2] I recommend that you add software quality to your KPIs and routinely track it. Quality is leading indicator: If it is decreasing, then you know that changing the product will become more and more difficult unless you do something about it. Knowing if and how much technical debt is building up helps you be proactive and avoid nasty surprises.

Roman Pichler

8.9 Working Software over Comprehensive Documentation

It is easy to miss the significance of the word "over" in the Manifesto. The four core statements are comparisons of things that are all considered valuable. The manifesto is often abbreviated to "Agile doesn't need [process, documentation, accountability, a plan]" but that is not what it says at all!

What it says is: "While we value [all of these things], we value these other things even more."

Working Software is a proxy for customer impact, Comprehensive Documentation is a proxy for delivery collateral. The

[2]https://en.wikipedia.org/wiki/Ward_Cunningham
[3]https://en.wikipedia.org/wiki/Martin_Fowler_(software_engineer)

former gives value now, the latter enables us to sustainably create value into the future.

"But," you say, "the code is the documentation! What more do you need?" Unfortunately code-as-documentation only answers one type of question: How did we decide to solve the challenge we had given the context and constraints at the time, and resources we had at our disposal?

It doesn't answer:

- What the context was or what those constraints were
- Who was involved
- How decisions were made, or who was involved in making them
- What other options we considered, and why we discarded them for this one
- How much autonomy the team had in building the solution
- How involved the various upstream, downstream, direct and incidental stakeholders were
- How happy we are with the solution we ended up with
- Which corners we cut deliberately, which shortcuts were forced on us, where we incurred debt by choice or by accident
- What we didn't know and found out later, and what we would have done differently if we had known

These are not just historical questions, they materially inform the present and future of any ongoing product development. Working Software is valuable right now. Comprehensive Documentation is valuable forever.

So given that we talk a lot about working software, what constitutes Comprehensive Documentation? Well the list of questions above is a good place to start, and one form of documentation that covers a lot of this is the Architecture Decision Record[4] or ADR. These come in various flavours, but they all have the same core goal of lightweight, version-controlled capture of point-in-time decisions that have a significant effect on a technology solution.

By looking at the date we can see when a decision was made, whether it superseded an earlier decision, how long the previous decision was in place for, and so on. You can also publish them into a team journal or blog so you create a narrative, rather than a wiki which does not have the same sense of time.

While we value Working Software, and everything else necessary to meet our customers' needs, we also value Comprehensive Documentation as a cornerstone of sustainability and continuity into the future.

Dan Terhorst-North

8.10 Montague Street Bridge

Melbourne is one of those cities where we think we are fairly special. We have our own 'culture' and, invariably, internet memes reflecting such culture.

One of the foremost Melbourne funnies is a meme about the Montague Street bridge which is an overhead traffic bridge carrying light-rail tracks (tram – yet another Melbourne cultural icon despite being available all over the world) over an inner city street called Montague Street.

---

[4]https://adr.github.io/

If you think, with a name like Montague, things are going to end up in tragedy, you'd be right. This bridge has a very low clearance of 3 metres and, as a result, high clearance vehicles such as buses and trucks have an unfortunate habit of running into it. There is even a website that hosts a 'number of days since accident' type counter that gets reset every time the bridge is hit. We are talking about the bridge being hit every one or two months on average, not to mention weekly multiple near misses.

As agile coaches, we work very hard on creating change and culture. But we cannot be successful working within the system that disallows change. There is no difference between an agile transformation rich in boundaries set against changing and death march projects. We cannot expect the onus to fall on the individuals to change when the organisation still operates within the old system that discourages change. As agile coaches, we help set the right environments for people to allow them to change, to make them want to change, change the work system that allows improvements but we cannot ever make people change.

Back to the Montague Street Bridge, we clearly have an issue with the system that expects the onus to change falling on individuals to change their driving behaviours. Of course, signages and warning systems have been employed to change the drivers' behaviours and yes, there have been some minor improvements. But the root cause of the problem, that the bridge clearance is unacceptably low, has never been addressed. We have data and evidence (in the form of internet memes, is there a better kind of evidence?) that despite all sorts of improvements done, accidents still happen on a regular basis. In fact, there was even a bus driver who was jailed for causing injuries to his passengers.

To truly change, transform and evolve, we must ensure that our change encompasses both the environment and the people - and this means we have to consider holistic changes to the structure, process, culture and people of our organisation as well as truly adapting to the change, and the resistance to our change, that will be thrown at us from our ecosystem - whether it comes from customers, partners, legislations or anywhere else.

After all, if the root cause of the crashes is the bridge and not the trucks, we must fix that bridge if we were to truly solve the problem.

Kanatcha Sakdiset

9. Customer collaboration over contract negotiation

9.1 Stop protecting your team

No too long ago, we worked with an awesome Scrum team. They knew everything there is to know about Scrum and had all the ceremonies down to a science, and despite having quite a few people leave the team and others join the team, something magical kept them together with a strong team feeling. It was their commitment to Scrum.

However...

This Scrum team worked on an app, that we can call Sonar and they needed the content for the app from the Retail department. Sonar would be nothing without it. The idea was for the app to interact with the customers in a very personal way saying things like "Hi, I am Sonar. I am your digital assistant" and they needed the "tone of voice" and visual design from the Digital Innovation department.

But...

The team – with the Scrum Master in front – was so busy working their Sprint backlog and keeping their velocity up, that they declined opportunity after opportunity to collaborate with their two main stakeholders, without whom Sonar would be a non-appealing and empty shell with zero business value.

When asked if they could go and work with their colleagues in Retail (who were seriously understaffed for this project – and who they could help by creating some content) or to reach out to other stakeholders in the organization, they first argued that this would jeopardize their sprint and destroy their velocity, and that second, it would need to wait until later, because "in Scrum we stick to the Sprint backlog once it is committed."

With tremendous effort from the organization around the team, we managed to help Retail create enough content and to get a good-enough tone-of-voice to get the Sonar app in the air with a couple of thousand beta-customers, and finally we were able to get some valuable feedback.

And then...

A few months later, when we paid them a visit to see how they were doing, the team had been closed down. Some of the team members had been laid off. Some – the most outgoing and service-oriented individuals – had been pulled into the Digital Innovation area. And the rest were more or less idle and orbiting around in the organization.

But they all (some now without a job) – with the Scrum Master in front – can proudly say, that they stuck to Scrum ;-)

We witness stories like this over and over again. Hopefully, soon the Scrum Masters who see it as their most important responsibility to protect their teams will realize that they need to shift their focus to do whatever is best for their companies and their customers.

Granted, there are situations where teams are hardly getting a chance to get anything done, because they are constantly interrupted by their stakeholders. If that is the case and if the Sprint backlog is more important for the business than the reasons for the interruptions, then it is a good idea for the Scrum Master, in close collaboration with the business stakeholders, to implement some sort of filter so only the most important interruptions reach the team members.

BUT for those of you Scrum Masters who believe that the Sprint backlog and the team velocity is always the most important... You need to pursue the bigger picture and proactively find out how your team can best contribute to achieve the overall business goals.

We're not saying you as Scrum Masters should have a totally open border (see A below) around your team, where any impulse around you will pass through and disturb the team all the time. But you should also not do the total opposite and create a border that is a thick shell (C) that can not be penetrated at any time during the Sprint. What you need to do is to find the right balance for your business context and create a diffuse-open border (B) around your team, so that the right amount of interaction with your stakeholders can happen.

Borders

So Scrum Master, stop protecting your team..

Instead, initiate collaboration between your team members and your stakeholders...about the stories in the next sprint...about what your team just finished in the current Sprint...about the next release...about anything that can make your team contribute better in the holistic view of creating business value.

Plan for weekly refining sessions where your team members interact with the business stakeholders.

Re-vitalize the Sprint Review, making sure to have both demo AND feedback on the agenda.

And help your team practice listening when receiving feedback, so your business stakeholders feel welcome and eager to – together with you – adapt your plan and your product to really benefit the business, to really delight your customers.

Building the right product and increasing business value can only happen through intense collaboration between all stakeholders – and that will only happen when you stop protecting your team.

Respectfully submitted by Ole Jepsen and Jenni Jepsen, goAgile
October 2018

9.2 Two simple heuristics that will solve (most of) the problems you face as a Scrum Master

I regularly hear about the problems Scrum Masters face. After more than 200 interviews with Scrum Masters in the

Scrum Master Toolbox Podcast, here are the 3 most common problems that we face in our work, in order of frequence):

- As a Scrum Master, I lack support from management, and when they don't actively fight Agile adoption, they are disengaged. This lack of engagement by managers undermines my work as a Scrum Master in many ways, for example: by giving permission to the team to release without testing properly, or to work in silos instead of collaborating with other teams.
- As a Scrum Master, I see Management starting Agile adoption because it is fashionable or "my friend's company also started it", or even worse: because the Board of the company mandated that we adopt Agile to deliver more, and faster. In other words, there's no Vision for the Agile adoption journey.

- As a Scrum Master, I try to get team members to collaborate, but they prefer to work alone and aren't able to see the problems they cause to other teams and other colleagues. I can see these systemic problems and their consequences, so I feel frustrated.

These are the most common "reasons" Scrum Masters see themselves failing and struggle to help the teams they work with, and ultimately the organizations they are there to help.

Can we really find simple approaches that help us tackle these problems?

I've come to value two very simple heuristics that have helped me either solve or cope with these problems. Before I describe my Scrum Master heuristics, let me tell you why they are so important. You see, my goal as a Scrum Master is simple: have

a positive impact on the people I work with.
Let me clarify that.

I don't think that my job is to save the team from the "big, bad management wolves" or to help the organization I work with become "successful". I've learned that those are impossible goals, and – most often – can lead us astray from our true mission: leave our environment a little better than we found it, by being an example of the change we advocate others to take.
As a Scrum Master, I succeed when other people around me feel that my presence has contributed to their success.
Roughly quoting Einstein: "try not to become a person of success but rather try to become a person of value."
Here are the heuristics I follow in my own work, which I believe help me tackle the 3 most common problems Scrum Masters face:
Don't shrink anyone, you are there to be of value, not to save people from themselves
Don't focus on safety, focus on impact. Help your team become a valuable team, not a safe haven for people who are afraid of growing.
Now for the two heuristics that help me in moments of doubt.

Vasco's Scrum Master Heuristic #1: Don't shrink anyone
I see many of my fellow Scrum Masters focusing on simple, yet elusive techniques. These techniques are there to either manipulate people into doing something they think is right or saving people from their own psychological traumas.

A simple example is when a Scrum Master tries to "make" team members collaborate who clearly are not mentally equipped to work in a collaborative environment.

Come closer. Just between you and me: not everyone is ready

to take on what it takes to be a team player. It's that simple!

Should you as a Scrum Master motivate, cajole and ultimately manipulate someone to "become" a team player? No!

Professional psychologists have looked into what are the characteristics and personality traits that help a person become a great team player. Some of those can be developed with the help of a professional, which you probably aren't!

However, some of these personal characteristics are innate to the individual – impossible to change.

Without the skills that psychologists develop over decades, it is nearly impossible to help people overcome the barriers to becoming a great team player.

My own checklist for great team players is below. But in simple terms: some people will always prefer to work alone. If that's OK in your environment, great! If not, then step back and let that person follow their path. Focus on the team instead! You are there to help the team grow, and sometimes that means growing out of a person's contribution.

A checklist for detecting great team players

- Offers help in the Scrum Daily, without wanting to force others to take their idea
- Accepts feedback, and recognizes contribution by others even when they disagree with the content of the contribution
- Challenges other's perspectives, but does not make that challenge a competition for the "only truth"
- Asks for help when in doubt if the Sprint Goal can be reached
- Accepts help when offered help by others

- Raises problems in meetings, and quickly focuses on finding possible solutions with the rest of the team
- Asks for a clear goal when the goal is not clear
- Sometimes, goes beyond the call of duty to deliver on a team-goal.

If you don't see at least 3-4 of these in a team member, then you may want to focus on those team members that have those behaviors! Remember, if you amplify collaboration and being a team player you will get more collaboration and more team players!

Vasco's Scrum Master Heuristic #2: Don't focus on safety, focus on impact

It is currently popular to focus on Psychologic Safety. Here's the thing. What's a safe environment for me may not be for another person.

Let me give you a concrete example.

As a senior developer gets challenged, that developer may receive that challenge as a gift. A tool to help them think through the problem in a deeper and more insightful manner. If the exact same challenge is delivered to a junior developer, that developer may feel their competence being challenged, rather than their proposal.

To some extent this is unavoidable. We all have insecurities that get triggered in some situations. So, my choice in these situations is simple: bring the discussion back to the goal of the team.

In practical terms, I try to help the team discuss and agree on their goal. The impact they hope to create. The goal for the team can be, for example, the Sprint Goal. And it is that goal that should be the driving force for the interactions. Not safety.

When the team believes in the goal they share, they are able to recover more easily from moments of temporary lack of safety. Remember, lack of safety is unavoidable to some extent.

The Ethics of the Scrum Master

These simple heuristics are not "right" (or wrong), they are simple guides that help me in my work when I have doubts or need to quickly react to a situation that the team faces or I face.

Heuristics like these are what will evolve the Scrum Master profession. Over time, I hope, we will develop a code based on real-world experiences, which may become a set of ethical standards.

One such ethical standard for me follows directly from the heuristics above: Don't try to act outside your domain of expertise. I'm no psychologist. If you are reading this, chances are you aren't either. So I choose to focus on my domain: collaboration with the aim to reach an explicit goal.

As a Scrum Master, my domain of expertise is collaboration!

Vasco Duarte

9.3 Collaboration

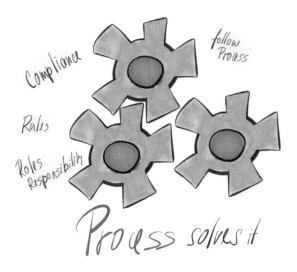

Process solves it

The traditional organizations are all about processes, rules, and delegation. All we need to do is to analyze the situation, come up with the way we want to handle it, and describe it in a process, and follow it. It shall be enough. It's the world where we simply rely on processes in our day to day decision making. In simple situations, it works well, as the transparency and predictability of the situation are playing in favor. In complicated situations, it might not be flexible enough and people and organizations will struggle to react properly to the situations. In a complex situation when it's hard to predict what happens it's mostly failing.

Tight processes are killing creativity and only work at simple and predictable situations.

I do it

The more complicated is the situation you face on day to day basis, the more are companies failing to describe the process to be followed. It seems to be unavoidable that rules and practices are not enough to be successful, delegation come in place and the situation results in creating new roles and position for those who are responsible for certain part of the process.

You do it

It allows more flexibility and responsiveness as people on the contrary to the processes can make a judgment based on the particular situation and solve it better. It's the world of individual responsibility, where we create a single point of contact we can blame when things go wrong. Similarly to the previews process-oriented world, there is no real collaboration happening. Either I do it, or you do it. And it must be clear who is the owner.

Individual responsibility kills collaboration and team spirit.

Finally, over here we cross the line of collaboration. At least from a technical point of view.

You help me

This already starts feeling like a collaboration.

At least at the first look, as there are more people working together. However, there is still one person responsible and the other just helping them.

I help you

It's a good first step, but at the end of the day, it's closer to the delegation scale, than collaboration as the unequal ownership make one side more invested in the results than the other, where the owner usually makes decisions, plans, and responsibility, while the other support them with the inputs. It's still more likely to create blaming than shared ownership and responsibility. While it may be a good first step, it's not collaboration as we speak about it in an agile environment.

Helping each other on their tasks is not a collaboration. Collaboration needs equal ownership.

Finally, there is a real collaboration, where people have shared responsibility, shared ownership, and one goal together.

We do it

It's not important who does what, there is no task assignment up front, they all just do what is needed and make their decisions at the time. This is a type of collaboration, is what makes teams in Agile and Scrum great. Such collaboration creates high performing environments. If you truly want to be agile, and not just struggle to pretend that following practices are enough, it's time to get rid of individual responsibility, which is often grounded in your org chart, position schemes, and career paths and learn how to create a real collaborative environment with shared responsibility and ownership. Learn how "We can do it together".

Zuzi Zuzana Sochova

9.4 There's no one-size-fits-all approach

I used to be a member of a women's gym. They put everyone on the same diet—no sugar, no carbs, high fat and high protein. I was so miserable on this diet! The sugar cravings were terrible and I would have seriously commited a crime for a piece of chocolate. Even worse, I didn't lose a pound!

When I started as a new Scrum Master, I knew what a good Scrum team should look like and I thought that if I just gave every team the same 'diet' they would learn too.

I soon discovered that just like every woman's body is different and has different needs, the same holds true for every Scrum team! They all have unique qualities and will learn at a different pace, even if they're part of the same company.

When you're working on changing the way people work, it's your job to push them to be better than where they are today, but at a pace that won't completely send them running down the street for a piece of chocolate (or a new job)!

I think of being a Scrum Master or agile coach a lot like my coach at the gym (that is the better one, that I now use)—you are there to make changes, but you need to understand the team, the individuals on the team and then nudge them along just a bit out of their comfort zone.

When you're trying to make changes to a team, it's natural to want to change everything at once, just like when you stop eating anything that tastes good and start working out at the same time—ouch, that's painful!

My advice to you is to prioritize change like you're asking the product owner to prioritize work. Find the small, easy wins that add the most value and implement those first. That will build up the team's confidence and willingness to go further!

Stacey Ackerman

9.5 Increase quality of meetings

This tip is based on the ESVP activity at funretrospectives.com. I have modified it by
removing anonymous aspect and making it more open.
As Scrum Masters we often face situations where some team members do not understand
the purpose of Scrum events. This is especially true for teams new to Scrum. One way to
address this is to work with people one on one and/or do a teaching session for the whole
team to increase the understanding. The other case could be that while everything seems to
be clear about Scrum itself, there are issues in the team like conflicts, poor dynamics that
make the team stale or look pale. This results in situations when some team members do
not want to collaborate, participate in Scrum events, etc. With the modified ESVP activity,
you can make the Scrum team help itself. And this is true also for other kinds of
teams/groups that are in need to work together.
Prepare four A4 size paper sheets each named accordingly to ESVP[1]. What is ESVP?
E=Explorer - person wanting to actively engage and collaborate with others. S=Shopper -

---

[1]http://www.funretrospectives.com/esvp-explorer-shopper-vacationer-prisoner/

person less active than Explorer, wanting to do less than Explorer. V=Vacationer - person

wanting to observe others doing. P=Prisoner - person rather being somewhere else or being

forced to come.

Let's assume Sprint Review is coming as the next Scrum event. When people have joined

the event, before even starting the Review, do the following: (1) say, let's do a small

warm-up/check-in and explain all for cards by showing them and putting each into own room

corner on the floor. It has to be done in a fun way without seriousness. Emphasize that this

is a safe, blame free, no judgement space. We are trying to improve our work together by

increasing understanding. Now, invite people to think about where they belong and to take

positions. (2) Now the interesting part starts. If 100% are E, then you are lucky and you can

proceed with the event - this is the easy case. If, however, you find Ps and/or Vs, the

discussion has to happen. Why? Because there are people in the room who either be

somewhere else or do not want to contribute. What can happen if part of audience is not

here and bored? So, the following has to happen: (3) first, kindly, with empathy in the whole

of you, invite Ps and Vs to tell about the reasons why they have put themselves in those

positions. You can also ask what could help them to move to another position? Discussion

may end here, but often needs to go on. (4) Ask the Es and Ss (depends if required) how

could they help Ps and Vs to change their positions. What could they suggest? If that is a
larger group, split them and timebox. In the meantime, talk to Ps and Vs in a coaching
stance. The goal of the above actions is to cause the dialog to happen between the different
sub groups in a safe manner.
In my experience, the above dialog about topics of this kind greatly enhances the quality of
the remaining event be it a Scrum Review, Retrospective or just another meeting. And not
just the event, but also the teamwork improves.

Ivo Peksens

9.6 Coaching teams: A journey of contradictions and context as a crucial driver

Coaches/consultants are often hired by organizations in an effort to transition/transform teams. Most times it's hard to understand the intent and the need given that the two words 'Transition' and 'Transformation' are used quite interchangeably. The meaning and the associated actions to carry out these are different. For ex. Instilling agile practices as a shift from other methods is different from shifting mindset, culture and behaviors to something better than the current state. A coach typically gets onboard with few initial discussions and presentations of potential approach. It's quite likely that a typical engagement begins where a coach/consultant spends sometime initially studying the ways of working in teams.

The desired expectations from coaching is shared by the management with some sense of the currents challenges and that of consultant's initial views which are sketched into what is likely the roadmap towards the stated goals or nirvana. This is where it all ends, the engagement with the teams and the situations or reality on the ground could be very different.

Let's step back a little and get a perspective on some of the contexts. We can broadly classify the context in each of People, Process and Tools & Technology areas.

People:

- Too many key stakeholders/bosses for a member
- Increasingly "Agile Process/Practices" encroaching upon new ideas/implementations/experimentations
- Agile has introduced more process and more managers, which is causing more confusion than before
- Some of the earlier coaching or expectations which asked Managers to move away from the mainstream ceremonies but are still responsible for other things ex. performance appraisals, hiring etc.
- Scrum Masters are messengers of PMs and lack of clarity in the new agile roles causing more distrust.

Process:

- Product backlog grooming sessions are ineffective and lack of skills/knowledge of effective slicing techniques.
- PMs, POs, Architects are giving directions that are often contradicting.
- PMs influencing the sprint backlog items without the knowledge of the PO

- High spillovers sprint over sprint
- Inaction on any of the action points from retrospectives

Engineering, Tools & Technology:

- Lack of tool adoption or ineffective usage of Devops tools chain.
- High technical debt and over engineering to implement solutions.
- Ineffective branching strategies and long lived branches leading to integration issues.
- Lack of skills using modern test automation tools and techniques.

Ravi Kumar

9.7 Since all those companies work Agile, we don't longer receive any commitment.

With frustration in his voice, this statement, aimed at a competitor, rolls out of the mouth of an external party that works together with different companies. Working Agile, in combination with an external party: is that possible? In my experience: Yes, it is possible, and I would make it even stronger: working with an external party can get smoother if we live the Agile principles and values.

What follows are practices that helped me out, working towards a goal together with an external party.

The basis for good cooperation is: trust, and adhere to agreements. So if you really cannot or do not want to give any commitment or forecast - and that applies to both supplier and customer - then things will not work out. Complete madness is totally not making a schedule with the excuse "we are Agile". You can always make the best guess and adjust it regularly. After a while you even get good at it. If you work together with a party other than your core team, which can be internal or external, it is essential to make a schedule and make proper agreements on this.

The ultimate advice on working with external parties is: look for the best way to communicate with each other as quickly as possible. Keep each other well informed. Evaluate that way regularly and make adjustments. What works for one party will not work for the other. Your communication (style) makes it best for you to depend on the culture and customs of the party you work with. I would like to give some tips that I think are useful in general:

- Tune as quickly as possible: eg from the moment you start designing a high level architecture.
- Search for who-to-whom to coordinate: Having one contact person is easy. For when you don't know where to go with a question, or as an "official channel". But letting everything pass through one person is anything but efficient or effective. For example, I do not see myself as the right person to discuss legal topics in detail. Tip: make sure there is one contact person on both sides, but also provide other links between both parties. Make sure that the contact person is informed at a high level of everything that is discussed between parties (for example, use your daily scrum for that).

- Tune regularly. Use as many existing Agile ceremonies as possible. My top experience is inviting an external party to your review: you are transparent and you give them the opportunity to receive feedback. Even though the party may not always be present: I have noticed the invitation is highly appreciated.
- Give feedback after the retrospective. During your retrospective, is something bubbling up with regard to the external party? Be sure to pass that on. Whether it is an appreciation or a point for improvement. Preferably a bit of both.

Not always everything goes well. Problems arise sooner or later. Shifting the blame on another does not solve a problem. If you are purely guided by the contract to determine who should solve something, then we are not working on good cooperation. I think it is important for everyone to see why something goes wrong. But the best solution can be built at the side that was not the source of the issue. You get far with goodwill on both sides. Sometimes one party will make extra effort, sometimes the other.

Do you not work with an external party? I predict that it won't take that long anymore, working with external parties will only increase. And as long as you only collaborate within your own company: use the above for your internal collaboration. Because in the end: external or internal collaboration, it doesn't make such a difference, right? Being skilled in good internal cooperation increases the chance of a good cooperation with an external party!

Nele Van Beveren

9.8 Building Client Trust

In 2015 before the NFL Superbowl[2], Seattle Seahawk player Marshawn Lynch[3] gave an interview where he responded to every question with, "I'm just here so I won't be fined." The moment a contract is in place, the motivation to approach meeting the contract details with the minimum enthusiasm is put in place. Some believe a contract will protect them from the worst case scenario, but don't consider that they are also avoiding the best case scenario. Time spent to perfect a contract is stolen from building a positive foundation for harmonious collaboration. Contracts are expensive and time consuming to enforce. Much of the peace of mind that comes from having a contract is more imaginary than practical.

I recently attended a meeting stressing the importance of showing our expertise, professionalism, and competence in client communication. I know we are good at what we do, and any mistakes we make do not change that. Being open about the unknown doesn't negate years of experience solving real problems. Reputation is based on the value we deliver overall. Clients care about what you can do for them. Showing progress does more for your reputation than anything you can communicate with words.

Our interactions either build trust, or erode it. When speaking to clients, engineers, or managers, there is only one message I mean to deliver with clarity: I am here to help you be successful. We are all people. If a customer feels the need to tell me, "I'm the client, and I am paying you, so you will do what I say," the relationship is in a difficult place. If faced

---

[2]https://en.wikipedia.org/wiki/Super_Bowl
[3]https://en.wikipedia.org/wiki/Marshawn_Lynch

with that kind of interaction, let unconstructive messages pass. Nothing that matters or lasts can be propped up by insincerity. Posturing to assert authority with a reminder of power, a mention of a contract, or a subtle threat comes at the cost of comfortable collaboration and flow.

It's difficult for clients to see possibilities without a working example. With a testable demo, we can confirm or refute our earlier assumptions and uncover new questions. Boundaries are real, and testable. For example, I'm never going to do something unethical, even if it costs a client or my job. Clear boundaries increase safety to collaborate. Be willing to clearly say no and explain why. Saying no is the only way that saying yes has value. Clients will test your demo and your boundaries. Show them the strengths and limitations of both in real time.

A lasting relationship that has been tested by both sides is more powerful than a contract. Some people are experts in using contract loopholes. Relationship loopholes can be closed in real time as needed. A relationship evolves and grows over time while a contract is only as good as your ability to predict the future. Choose the relationship.

Lanette Creamer

9.9 Agile Coaching Agreement as Creative Partnership

What Makes Us Coachable

Once I was asked what the most important aspect is that makes a person or a team coachable. My response was: "Being at choice". Remember those situations when someone decided what's best for you? Even with the best intent, how did it make you feel? How did it impact the sense of your own capabilities and your commitment to such a decision? Furthermore, how did your relationship change when you were not even asked to participate in decision-making about something important to you?

In many ways we are the choices we make (and not making a choice is also a choice). One cannot fully take ownership of the change unless they treat it as the choice they made. Now think about the times when you as an Agile coach might have made decisions for the teams or individuals. How did that land? Especially in the long-run? Did the change stick? Did it fully yield the benefits you were hoping for?

From my experience impactful coaching follows 3C's - it starts with a Choice to take a Chance to make a Change. Curiously enough, impactful coaching results in new 3C's - in making new Choices, discovering novel Chances and bringing different Changes. I imagine it to be the ever-expanding and evolving loop of our development.

However let's not be delusional, being at choice does not necessarily mean you are going to like the options you have. Yet choosing between uncomfortable and unpleasant, difficult and scary, unknown and potentially painful, does not take away your freedom of choosing your attitude.

Once you start perceiving reality through the lens of choices, new opportunities for changes become available - for you and for others. Choice is always there, whether we notice it or not. The biggest irony is that the Universe will keep bringing us in similar situations and making us face similar challenges until we learn to make new choices.

Coaching Agreement Is about Framing Our Choices

How do we frame our choices as we start the Agile coaching

journey? Having an open and honest conversation about expectations in the beginning of a coaching relationship can be hard. Main focus is usually on the choice of methods, frameworks and metrics. It is often expected of an Agile coach to do their "magic", and of the teams to follow or be "served". Coaching goals are frequently cascaded top-down and formulated with an implicit message to "fix" people and processes in the hope that it will improve performance, culture, customer centricity, overall organisational ability to respond to change, etc. We tend to shy away from discussing many uncomfortable questions at the start, and thus miss critical points of framing our choices, which inevitably leads to misalignment in expectations on all sides, resistance and pain for everyone involved. "Somehow we'll sort it out" is not a reliable strategy, and "we'll do it later" in my experience is always way too late.

But what if we could do it differently? What if we start every Agile coaching engagement with explicitly outlining expectations, boundaries, coaching goals and other choices? In Agile transformations contexts it's rarely easy but it's always worth it.

Coaching agreements are the starting point on the path towards the development of a coaching program in the world of professional coaching. They are based on the Code of Conduct and clearly state areas of responsibility. In the Agile world there is a growing number of initiatives and overall trends in "professionalizing" Agile coaching, yet there are very few guidelines to support the creation of Agile coaching agreements in practice.

Agile Coaching Agreement Dimensions

So what do I mean exactly when I say Agile coaching agreement? The following list could never be exhaustive (because of unique contexts we all operate in), but it can give you some ideas on the clarity we are trying to gain in the dimensions of:

- Coaching Relationship:
  - what Agile coaching is and is not (e.g., it is eye-level collaboration and it's not performance management)
  - what is and is not appropriate in the relationship (e.g., open and honest feedback is appropriate, and sharing confidential information without consent is not appropriate)
  - what is and is not being offered (e.g., an Agile coach is offering coaching support for the teams and individuals to discover and unlock their potential, and an Agile coach is not offering psychotherapy and working with traumas)
  - the responsibilities of the parties involved (including an Agile coach, the team, sponsor and other stakeholders)...
- Coaching Process:

- guidelines and specific parameters such as logistics, scheduling, duration, milestones, termination, confidentiality and inclusion of others...

- Coaching Plan and Goals:
  - including the alignment between the goals from the sponsor, other relevant stakeholders and the team
- Team-Coach Compatibility:

- an explicit decision by the team and the coach that it's a "match" that both sides are willing to explore further

Why Agile Coaching Agreement?

One might wonder why we need to spend time on discussing and deliberately making decisions on the points above. After all, don't actions speak louder than words? Skipping this part might seem rational for those very outcome- and action-focused, yet it will inevitably result in friction and tension down the road. You choose! :)

Let me share with you the "why's" of Agile coaching agreements I noted during my past 10+ years of hands-on coaching and being coached myself:

- As mentioned above, gaining clarity on expectations and potential coaching scope will help you define if this engagement is a good fit for you, and if you're good fit for it

- Having a conversation about 'what is' and 'where next' can raise awareness of all parties about existing (potentially unaddressed) needs. Sensing into the needs and linking them to the requests is a good exercise to ensure alignment and coherence

- Co-creating and capturing coaching goals will help you keep focus on the right things and prioritise accordingly

- Start growing trust through transparency of your coaching agenda (in the service to and on behalf of the goals) from day one

- Ensuring that all voices are included into your coaching agreement supports psychological safety and openness to experiments

- Having an explicit coaching agreement in place cultivates ownership of the development by individual contributors, teams and leaders (your coaching clients are using your coaching service to achieve their goals)

- By openly discussing what teams and leaders are hoping to gain from Agile coaching, you are nurturing commitment to change and foster taking responsibility

- Coaching agreement has proven to be indispensable in quickly establishing healthy boundaries and making necessary distance in the service of greater objectivity

- Building partnership relationship with your coaching clients - whether teams, leaders or individual contributors - allows for the depth of conversations you could never imagine possible

- Co-creating Agile coaching agreement is a dynamic activity inviting everyone to explore their edges (yes, your edges as a coach, too!)

- I often think about the Agile coaching agreement practice as a litmus test for further coaching engagement - e.g., if teams or leaders are not willing to commit to try something new and expect an Agile coach to do all the "work" for them, what are the chances they will be open for new (Agile) ideas and concepts?

- Co-creating, refining and discussing an Agile coaching agreement is a great opportunity for the teams and stakeholders to experience your coaching in action (yes, it starts there!)

- And last but not least, on the days when things do not go so smoothly, and you start questioning your choices as a coach, coming back to the agreement helps you stay grounded in your coaching intent

No Triangulation Rule

It's extremely important to mention here the so called "no triangulation" rule, meaning that for the coaching approach to be in integrity with its very essence, the relationship between the coach, their clients (individuals or groups) and involved stakeholders (e.g., sponsor or managers) should never involve:

- seeking for indirect obtaining viewpoints and observations from others (e.g., coach asking a sponsor in a private conversation what complaints they have about teams)

- sharing your personal experience of coaching individuals and groups with third parties unless you acquired explicit consent from your clients (e.g., coach sharing with a manager that a few teams complain about their behaviour)

- acting on behalf of such information without first-hand exploration (e.g., coach changing the way they treat a team member based on the feedback from a stakeholder, without having inquired about possible issues)

Triangulation brews hidden agendas, erodes trust, creates silos and unhealthy boundaries, supports spreading rumours and gossip, and eventually fuels into internal turf wars and backstabbing politics. Triangulation conversations might look and feel innocent, as a "water cooler" talk and office news exchange. Don't get caught in the middle. Simply put, do not talk about others behind their backs.

A few tips you might find helpful for "collapsing the triangle":

- proactively share "no triangulation" principle at the start of your engagement

- if somebody starts discussing someone not present in the room, stop the conversation

- encourage exploring alternatives to triangulation, model healthy direct communication and even constructive conflict

- suggest to bring the issue into the common meeting

"No triangulation" rule fully applies to Agile coaching agreements. Most often it would mean to have a team and a sponsor in one space getting aligned on their needs and goals.

Final Tips

"Courage doesn't happen when you have all the answers. It happens when you are ready to face the questions you have been avoiding your whole life". - Shannon L. Alder

I remember how nervous I was many years ago when suggesting to co-create an Agile coaching agreement for the first time. I didn't have all the answers, I didn't know where the conversation would take us. I knew however that I needed to bring up many questions that would either make people in the room uncomfortable or surprised, or both. Stepping into such conversation simultaneously holding the perspectives of openness and my personal choices integrity, was essential to invite a powerful transformation space of a creative partnership.

Here are some final practical tips to support you in designing your Agile coaching agreements:

1. Get clear on your values, principles and intent, and agree on the "rules of the game" before you start the Agile coaching engagement
2. Co-create your introduction as an Agile coach together with a sponsor
3. Use transactional and relational approaches when appropriate (not every engagement should and can be relationship-based, sometimes transactional approach is sufficient)
4. Share the questions to be discussed about Agile coaching agreement with the sponsor and the team in advance
5. Regularly review and adjust your Agile coaching agreement

May your choices reflect your hopes, not your fears. - Nelson Mandela

Nadezhda Belousova

10. Responding to change over following a plan

10.1 Love your customer

Working well together as a team is great. Working well together as a team to create products that make our customers awesome, is AMAZING!
No matter how good the team is, if it is not working closely with the customer to understand their needs it will build products and solutions that are not valuable. It will not relieve a pain and will not offer an opportunity for the customer to be competitive and a leader in their market.

A Scrum Master observes the connection the team has with the customer and enables an environment that makes this connection richer. Let's make sure the Product Owner meets the customer regularly. Let's make sure that Product Owner brings other team members to these meetings. UX, QA, Dev, Analysts... they all collaborate better and bring better solutions when they see how the customer uses the product, what frustrates them, and what they love. Bring your customers to your team, get to know people by name, show them what you are working on, listen to their feedback and ask if you can meet them again soon. Help to create personas that the team relates to and make these personas always visible when you plan, when you make decisions, and when you celebrate.

The team is less resistant to accept a change from the initial plan when they relate it to the pain the customer is having. The team will not resist creating a new plan when they understand the customer needs to respond to competition quickly. The team will ASK for a change on the plan when they see opportunities for better customer experience. It is no more a "scope creep" discussion but rather a discussion about improving our product to give our customers better tools to achieve their success.

By loving the customer, the team is more aligned and more focused on what they do. They understand the "why" behind every story they prioritize. They become story tellers instead of requirement followers. They become advocates of the product inside and outside of your company. They become PROUD of what they do.

The best places I have worked at have been those where people worked together, supported each-other, had fun, and they were proud of their products. The hallways were full of posters that showcased how the customers used the products and how the customer was awarded and recognized for doing an amazing work using our products. We enabled the creativity of our customers and they created masterpieces.

Love your customers and help your team to fall in love with your customers too.

Ardita Karaj

10.2 Enable Growth

I find myself playing a mix of the scrum master and product owner roles when supervising my research project students to balance student learning/growth with expected project outcomes. As a good supervisor (or research scrum master), I want to enable them to discover their own talents at research and grow during the project. At the same time, factors such as the project duration and outcome expectations come into play. For example, in a typical PhD project, there is plenty of time to allow the student to pick up personal and professional skills, grow their autonomy, and prepare them as independent researchers and potential future colleagues. In shorter research projects, e.g. a summer project, there is far more time pressure to focus and achieve the project objectives. I find myself adapting my approach to suit the context of the project.

I also find that the needs of individuals vary based on their own personalities/backgrounds, previous research experience (if any), expectations, dedication, attitude to learning, and more. In response, my approach to being their scrum master also varies. I try to provide support appropriate to the individual's needs. Sometimes being rather instructional and hand-holding in the initial stages, e.g. for students with no prior research experience. For more mature students, this approach evolves to being empowering, asking questions, helping them figure out their own solutions, being a sounding board for ideas, pushing their limits, challenging their favourite 'go-to' practices etc.

What I enjoy the most is to see them grow in autonomy, experience, expertise and innovation. Each student is unique and I have to customize my approach accordingly. It is a challenging but rewarding experience.

Rashina Hoda

10.3 The evolutionary path from authority to agility

In the 16th century, a revolution was beginning in Europe. The change was to affect how, around the world, we solve problems and make decisions. Up until the beginning of the upheaval, people looked to authority, at that time, the authority of kings and the church, to make decisions about pretty much everything. Now, moving forward, the message was, use evidence and logic to think about the solution. Reliance on the scientific method instead of following orders was life-changing. It still is. We seem to keep fighting this battle on all fronts. It seemed remarkable that a group of revolutionaries could apply this approach to software as recently as February 2001. To declare, among other principles, that we should respond to change over following a plan, is nothing less than a vindication of scientific thinking. There are many reasons why I am an agile follower, but the primary one has to be that I also believe it is the best approach (so far) to intellectual challenges. It's paradoxical, then, to realise that we have no proof for this. We say we "believe" that science will find the answers or that agile is the best approach, but where is the "proof" for this belief? I think this means that these are early days. We might believe that we have made enormous progress since the 16th century, and indeed we have, but if we look at the "science" of medicine, for example, we will see that physicians used blood-letting for over 2,000 years, "believing" that it was best practice. This "best practice" was responsible for countless unnecessary deaths, including that of the first president of the United States, George Washington. How many software projects have failed as a result of the equivalent of project blood-letting? Is it still going on? You're smiling, aren't you? So am I. I guess we're not there yet, but we hope and believe that we are on the right path.

Linda Rising

10.4 Bypassing Binary Thinking for Better Understanding

As a Scrummaster or Agile Coach, your job is mostly interacting with other people. Your job is helping those people do the bestthat they can do, and part of that is certainly helping them understand what is possible. That's why you'll receive so many tips
on what you might tell them.

There's another aspect that is perhaps even more important. That's the aspect of what you can hear from those same people. You cannot help them freely make good choices if you cannot understand what they are thinking and feeling. To understand that, you must not only listen to the words they say, but to the meaning that they give to those words. And the words that they say may mean something different from your point of view than it does from theirs. Misunderstandings are likely, and those misunderstandings will interfere with your work.

If you are trying to get someone to understand an Agile way of working and they're accustomed to some other approach, then thethings that they say may depend on implicit understanding

of their experience that you don't share. If you then interpret them according to your implicit understanding of Agile, the message may be mangled
or lost. While misunderstandings can get very subtle, many of them are pretty easy to detect by the fact that what they say makes no sense to you. So you seek a meaning that you can understand. "Since what they said makes no sense, they must mean this."

Beware, for this is a trap. This trap will have you believe your first interpretation that does make sense to you, and you'll stop there. Notice that you have two interpretations—one that can't possibly be right and another that, therefore, must be the right one. Become sensitive to having two interpretations, and let that trigger you to think of the
Rule of Three.

Virginia Satir expressed the rule of three that having one choice is no choice, having two is a dilemma, and having three is a choice.
At these moments of interpreting something that makes no sense, I like Jerry Weinberg's
formulation. If I can't think of three interpretations of this, then I haven't thought about it enough.

Of course, it may be that my first interpretation is correct. I often find, however, that I quickly reach two interpretations— one I prefer and another that makes that one look good in comparison. But before I select that preferred interpretation, I push myself
to find a third.

Sometimes it's very hard to find that third interpretation. But when I do, I often find I've found a fourth, a fifth, and perhaps many more in quick succession. I've broken the mental logjam of looking at things in a binary fashion and can see myriad possibilities.

It's then that I have a choice of how I interpret what the other person is saying. That choice greatly increases my chances of understanding correctly. And if I'm still puzzled, I can ask better questions in order to understand.

George Dinwiddie

10.5 Going Viral

An inefficient virus kills its host. A clever virus stays with it.
-James Lovelock

I was talking with a friend the other day about that magical time you experience when you first start with a company. You know, it's that honeymoon period where you feel like everything you do is effective. People are nice to you, things are easy, the company feels like someplace you can make a difference. You are on top of the world. Things just work.

Of course it doesn't last. After a while, for some reason it gets harder and harder to create change – to do something new. People don't think those ideas sound all that novel anymore. Getting things done starts to feel slow and laborious. Soon you are just another one of the gang. Part of the status quo.

If you are a consultant, perhaps it's time to declare victory and move on. After all, the average consulting contract isn't that long. Perhaps only 6 months. You introduce some change and then leave before things get too tough. That's a good thing too, because before long, they're on to you.

So what is happening here? I have a theory. It's a little whacky, but hear me out: I think that a workplace is a living system and that when a new person joins it's kind of like introducing a virus. The system, the corporate entity, doesn't know how to handle it. It doesn't recognize it. It doesn't know how to react. So the virus...er...person, simply by their very existence, provokes a reaction in the system. Of course living systems adapt. Slowly sometimes, but they do adapt. After six months or so, you are no longer an unknown virus. The antibodies in the system have learned to react to your novel behavior. You are no longer novel to the system. You are part of the system. That is good and bad. It's not all bad being part of the system. But you may find that its now really hard to get the same level of response to ideas for change. After all, they've heard it before. You are now a known quantity.

So what do you do? Move on? What if you aren't a consultant? Well we know the system reacts to a novel inputs. You are no longer novel, so...you have to make yourself into something novel if you expect to create a similar impact to when you first joined. You must make yourself into something new and different that the system doesn't expect.

You must change.

If you want to change the system you need to change yourself. Otherwise the system will recognize you and will fail to react. You need to change your behavior, so that the system has to adapt to your new behavior. You don't ask others to change. You change yourself and the system will change to adapt to you.

Tom Perry

10.6 Eliminate comparison and encourage progress

Have you ever felt demotivated when you are trying to change habits or work towards a goal and don't see instant results? Is it intimidating and uncomfortable because you are you comparing yourself to your desired end state? Teams going through agile transformations endure the same cycle of emotions. Based on how we perceive our environment, our brain secretes neurochemicals that can keep us motivated or demotivate us from making progress. Basic neuroscience shows that creating a comfortable environment by focusing on small incremental progress is the key to becoming a great team.

The twelfth principle of the Agile Manifesto states, "At regular intervals, the team reflects on how to become more effective, then tunes and adjusts its behavior accordingly." Teams often start with defining their "perfect" state and start making changes to achieve their goals. How do they define "perfect"? The same way many of us do. We have a frame of reference and in this case the frame of reference is high performing teams. A common phrase from management and Agile Practitioners is "I want us to be self-organizing and accountable like Spotify teams." These comparisons distract us and our team from making incremental goal oriented progress. When teams compare themselves to others, they can easily become frustrated and stressed. Science shows that the brain releases a neurochemical called cortisol when stress levels are increased.

In an article titled Cortisol: Why the "Stress Hormone" Is

Public Enemy No. 1[1], Christopher Bergland explains that "Cortisol is released in response to fear or stress by the adrenal glands which can interfere with learning, memory, and a slew of other things." When experimenting to improve the current process, assessing past iterations helps determine what to change. Teams learn from what was done and make a hypothesis on what will make them them better. Raised cortisol levels are are a problem because they are demotivating. They provide an environment where the question "why are we not good enough" is the focus instead of "how can we become better?" Essentially, we want to avoid stressful environments by removing comparisons.

So how can teams improve? They need to ask, "what is better than our current state?" instead of, "what is our desired end state?".

Encouraging a team to focus only on themselves and make small incremental changes is a key to success. Comparison is a distraction. Seeing the completion of goals accomplished in short intervals is satisfying. The feeling of satisfaction motivates teams to continue making progress and deliver faster results. When feeling good, the brain once again gets involved by releasing a chemical called dopamine.

Psychology Today defines dopamine[2] as "a neurotransmitter that helps control the brain's reward and pleasure centers. The euphoric feeling keeps people motivated, enables teams to see rewards, and take action to move toward them." Unlike the stress chemical cortisol, dopamine releases enable them to continuously stay motivated. Although the gratification is not always instant, it is fast enough to show teams they are

---

[1]https://www.psychologytoday.com/us/blog/the-athletes-way/201301/cortisol-why-the-stress-hormone-is-public-enemy-no-1

[2]https://www.psychologytoday.com/us/basics/dopamine

making progress.

Agile practices such as retrospectives create an environment where teams see the reward of their gradual improvements and stay motivated. Retrospectives consist of improvement experiments, which are easier to analyze when there are shorter feedback loops. The approach is similar to the "fail fast" mindset. It is easier to fix bugs and stabilize software when issues are detected and fixed early on. In essence, a retrospective helps analyze what isn't working in shorter cycle and helps teams find faster fixes. In the end, the motivated team becomes highly productive through continuous improvements.

Becoming a great agile team is easy with the right mindset and environment. Remove the focus from being like other desirable teams and focus on the team at hand.The next time a team says they want to perform at a desired level, ask first, "what can we realistically do to make things better tomorrow?"

Hina Popal

10.7 Things happen in their own time

What type of person picks a relatively new career like "Scrum Master"? A role that often involves working in organizations that transition to agile and go through lots of uncertainty. A role that focuses on "inspect and adapt", e.g. change. What type of person indeed? Probably a person that is curious and excited to try new things. Does that sound like you?

Here's the thing though, different people have different degrees of "eagerness to try stuff out". As a Scrum Master you are likely very near the "Yay, let's try this"-end of the scale. Which means that most of the other members in the team will be closer to the "tried and true"-end scale than you, i.e. less eager for change.

It can be frustrating if you can hardly wait to experiment while others want to wait and see. At least it was for me. I was sooo impatient. Why didn't the others feel the same urgency and thrill I did?

I've since realized that things happen in their own time. We're asking people to think and act in a new way after they've been seeped in the "traditional" way for years and years. That takes time. You can only help people with what they are ready to hear and with the problems they are aware they're having. Nowadays, instead of pushing harder against ever-increasing resistance, I'm planting seeds – ideas for what the team can try. Sometimes the team runs with something right away, sometimes
they come back to a suggestion after weeks, sometimes they come up with a different solution, sometimes the problem goes away. All of these are fine.

So please don't beat yourself up (or forcefeed the team) if things don't seem to move fast enough. Remember that they are likely not on the samepage. Yet. Be patient, sow the seeds and be there to water the seedling when it breaks out of the soil towards the sun.

And the best of all: Change is like a muscle. The more new things you try out as a team, the easier it gets. Eventually big changes become easy.

Corinna Baldauf

10.8 Where did governance go?

How many times have we heard the story - "super large global multinational organisation going agile" - and the transformation failing to deliver on its goals? Or the "175 year old traditional banking and finance organization designing its agile transformation by adopting tribes and squads and copying Spotify" - and then realising that the wrong work is getting prioritised locally, we have no visibility of the work or system of work, and every tribe has a two year plus planned backlog meaning no ability to **Respond to Change**? Not very agile is it. What's gone missing?

Governance can be defined for the purpose of agile as how an organisation controls the making of its decisions - what systems, culture, norms, behaviours and structures are in place that lead to decisions and outcomes. These generally evolve naturally and in response to problems to be solved over time, as an organisation goes through its own lifecycle. Often large organisations attempt agile and business transformation efforts to change these underlying variables - yet many do not purposefully address their governance system as an area of concern, and the system ends up reverting to what it was prior to the transformation effort. We don't address or encourage change in the control levers.

Agile evolved from the world of the small team - it's powerful, successful and leads to better outcomes. The agile revolution has proven this, and many of the Tips in this book will attest to that. Where agile has struggled is when we apply the small team thinking to an organisational lens, without taking into account the different risk profiles of participants, decision making complexity and problems to be solved. Even the much vaunted spotify model (yes I do agree this is not a model) has "anecdotally" struggled across tribes. One organisation I have worked with had this problem - when jobs to be done evolved from ideas to demand, there is often an inability to link across multiple agile teams collectively and collaboratively. If we fail to realign governance to the needs of agile teams we are amplifying the feedback loops we dont want - and potentially we introduce delivery risk. we need to change the way we control - from controlling decisions, to controlling how decisions are made instead.

We need to rethink governance and what control means. Who's working on what, is it aligned strategically, is it the right work, and how do we know - which always were important questions - demand a different approach. Effective agile governance enables autonomy with directional alignment : Agile Governance applies the principles of agile as first described in the Agile Manifesto to the whole of the organisation and how it designs the mechanisms by which it can execute and control its strategies.

We can narrow agile governance down to four key themes, or pillars I think you need to effectively govern an agile system of work and ensure the right controls are in place:

- **Radical transparency**: The key to agility lies in the speed at which information flows around the organisation, followed by how this information is used in decision making. Transparency is an essential component of speed and also a key enabler to building trust between people and teams. Share everything. Often.
- **Systems of work**: A key to high performing teams using agile methods is the ability for the teams to describe their own local "way of working" and create a safe

space for ideas to flourish. Distribute this control - move away from mandated process and stage gating of work, and focus on high level intent that you ask people to consider. Governance becomes more about "have" they designed for work, rather than "auditing compliance to" the design of work.

- **Data analysis**: Working in agile methods requires different ways of understanding where teams are in terms of their predictability, delivery and improvement over time. Use data dynamically from source systems to form insights - move away from 100 page static status reports. Fact over opinion.

- **Intent based leadership**: Modern agile ways of working require a style of leadership that moves from the mechanistic approach where people are viewed as cogs in a machine, where tasks are allocated, to one where creativity and individualism can flourish. Agile methods need leaders who support, guide and provide enabling constraints rather than try and control with preventative ones. Ensure you don't govern process and tasks, but instead, outcomes and engagement. Distribute control.

Agile works. It changes the way you think about work. And for agile to succeed in large scale organisations, it needs a rethink of governance to sustain it. Adopt lightweight governance using the same underlying values that makes agile work.

Phil Gadzinski

10.9 "RI" Mode Sprint Planning

It is about a "SHU HA RI" story of Sprint Planning. If you are having a 2 weeks Sprint, it is likely that you might be doing a 4 hours Sprint Planning on day-1 of a Sprint. This is a "ShU" level of a Sprint Planning.

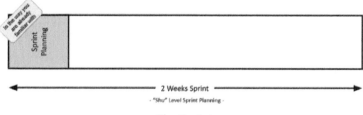

Shu Sprint

At the "HA" level, you begin learning from many sources about practices on how to conduct Sprint Planning until you meet the practices that fit for your team at the current time.

Short story, Your product is growing and accepted by the market. Your team is overwhelmed with customers requests. The Product Owner gets difficulty to maintain the schedule of the Sprint Planning. After a Retrospective, the team decides to change the time of when they can do a Sprint Planning. Your team comes with the new way of doing a Sprint Planning (a "RI" level).

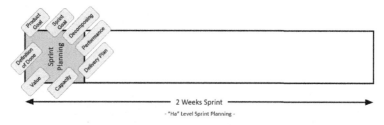

Ha Sprint

The benefits of splitting the Sprint Planning can be that the Product Owner has slightly easier to attend the Sprint Planning, some plans might be changed or refined as more information comes, and the team could get more information on how likely they are able to deliver the increment and the value considering the empirical data they got so far.

Ri Sprint

Ivan Darmawan

10.10 Love is key

I love people. I am passionate about them. As a Scrum Master, when I get into the office in the morning, I think to myself: "Wow, what a great bunch of people!". And then I put all my energy into improving the system to allow the greatness of these people to do its magic. This is what gets me soaring when things go well, and what keeps me going when they are tough.

In 2020 things were tough. In March 2020, worldwide governments shut down onsite collaboration when the first pandemic of our lifetime spread – and suddenly, we were at home. By that time, I had been with my team for only a couple of weeks, and our big quarterly planning meeting was rapidly approaching. And suddenly we found ourselves at home, struggling to connect to the internal network of our workplace. Not allowed to share sensitive information via private technology, but the professional, secure environments not being ready for us. One of the first days, it took us 4 hours before we were in a shared call with the whole team. Yet we needed to continue our value delivery. And our planning. And our team development. But the toughest problem was that I felt responsible for everything that did not work properly. I felt I needed to be the glue for my team that kept them together and the beacon of light that would guide them through that time. While struggling just as much as them at the same time. For a while I even considered to quit and to apply for a job in a supermarket instead, where at least it would be clear what would be expected of me. After the weekends I dreaded going back to work, and the weeks went by in a blur: **never really experiencing a time-out, yet also never experiencing a flow.**

Then I had enough of the complaining. I decided that this was the new normal for now and that I was going to take proper care of myself first, no matter the consequences. I decided that I was allowed to take breaks and NOT be available for questions or information. I decided that whatever we managed to do was an incredible win. And that whatever we did not manage to do was not due to my personal incapability to support the team (yes, I am talking to you, Imposter Syndrome!).

This turned out to change the situation profoundly: I started worrying less about our progress and process and instead **checking in more with my team members on a personal level**. To allow myself to enjoy these interactions. To make sure I would have some informal 1:1 contact every day, be it after a meeting when still aligning with one person about something or be it in deliberately dropping a chat message. I allowed myself to be less efficient about working from home.

And that was indeed a turning point: As a team we grew tightly together, professionally as well as personally. **And we delivered. Every Sprint, our energy grew, and alongside the satisfaction and appreciation of our stakeholders.**

In the meantime, our environment kept changing: We lost our tester – so we started a test automation ambush of a dimension that I have never seen before. We gained 2 new team members – so we started regular pair or mob programming, peer reviews and innovation sessions. All of this was hard work, but the astonishing thing is: it all just happened while we were enjoying ourselves and focusing on the next concrete step to go. By now I can honestly say that I've never in my life been part of a team as successful and powerful as this.

Here is the lesson that I learned last year: although over the years I have built up a great toolkit with knowledge on Scrum, SAFe, LeSS, Agile, Project Management and a ton of facilitation and coaching techniques, the real miracles start happening when I allowed myself to invest time and energy to love my team and each of my team members. With all my heart. Unconditionally. Fiercely.

It is this love that makes me alert for the real issues on the root of the problems at hand. It is this love that gives me the courage to act on our problems, even if they are huge and if the solution is messy and ugly or (even worse) not clear. It is this love that allows me to put my full cognitive and emotional capacity out there. That ignites a desire to learn, about myself, about my team members and about the new situation that every new day presents us with.

We care about our product and about our team. We talk to each other and have a genuine desire to improve and learn. We run experiments and build new practices and habits. **And THAT is what it takes to make an amazing team. And an amazing team will deliver amazing products,no matter what tools they get and no matter what process they use.**

How can you apply this to your own context?

I can encourage you to practice loving yourself and loving your team(s). It can be small steps.

- You feel a drop in your energy?

  Take a break. Your problem will still be there afterwards. You cannot muster the discipline to take a break? Schedule a break in your calendar, maybe invite someone else to trigger more external pressure. E-mails or meetings are diluting your focus? Make appointments with yourself where you only focus on one topic. Block your calendar.
- There is a problem that you just can't solve?

Talk to someone. You feel a spike in your energy as a reaction to a colleague? Let them know of the effect they have on you!

- You see your team struggle with a problem?

Stop what you are doing for a moment and offer your empathy and your support. Find the learning opportunity in the problem and celebrate it with them.

These are just a few examples – in the end love is a very personal concept, and what triggers love for me or how I spread this love might be very different from you. And that is the beauty of this tip: you do not need me or a manual or anyone else to apply it.

You already have everything that you need inside you!

Go out, share your love – and you'll be surprised of its powerful effect, no matter whether at home, at work or just anywhere in life.

Anke Maerz

10.11 Agility =/= Speed

I was changing a lightbulb this morning and was struck by a shift that has occurred in recent years. Lightbulbs used to be sold according to their power consumption. People were entrained to buy bulbs according to power rating — what the bulb consumed from the electrical grid — rather than brightness — what they, as consumers, actually benefited from.

Filament bulbs are incredibly inefficient, producing more heat than light — which certainly has parallels in many discussions in software development. It is not simply that old bulbs were inefficient, but that this inefficiency was both stable — the brightness of 60 W bulbs changed little over decades — and expected. The expectation reinforced the idea that efficiency would not improve. It was an expectation that masked many assumptions and created secondary industries, such as lava lamps. Delightful as they are, the only reason that lava lamps were ever a thing is because lightbulbs produced so much waste heat.

The problem is clear and, had we been able to look past our assumptions, it was always clear. Brightness is measured in lumens. A whole industry was built on having people buy according to the wrong measure. For as long as it was stable and widely used, it was unquestioned and acted as a suitable proxy. But in the presence of change, people have found they are so accustomed to using the wrong measure that they struggle to know what they actually want using the right measure. It is common for modern energy-saving bulbs to be sold by lumens accompanied by an old wattage equivalent.

In software development, a discipline built on abstraction, we should be wise to this phenomenon... but all too often we fall into it. Marketeers and advertisers talk about 'engagement' metrics for websites, but the one thing their metrics do not actually measure is engagement. Product owners are encouraged to 'prioritise by business value', when such an approach is impossible within the laws of physics as we currently understand them — by all means prioritise by estimated business value, but don't fool yourself into thinking that an estimate is an actual. Teams that aspire to be more agile have created currencies of story points and have ritualised development velocity. They have mistaken a weak proxy measure as a meaningful system of estimation, indication of progress and mark of quality. This is not agility.

An obsession with speed often overtakes the core values of agile software development. It's not just the development of software; it's the development of working software. And we should be cautious of any language or technique that optimises around project management measures. Software development is better thought of in terms of product development than project management, therefore time to market is typically less important than time in market. Sprinting matters less than endurance.

Sprints are not about sprinting

Our thinking about business and the business of software is framed in terms of the language we use. Sometimes our words and metaphors can hinder just as much as they can help. For example, when Scrum originally adopted the word sprint in the early 1990s, it was to contrast it with the word iteration. At the time, when people spoke of iterative and incremental development, iterations could be months long — objectives would meander and scopes would drift. By contrast, the word sprint suggested an activity that was directed, short and uninterrupted. This was the original sense and, for its time, it had value.

Times change and time changes everything, including our words. The mechanics of software delivery have become fine grained to the point of continuous. The intended distinction between sprint and iteration is long gone; the residual meaning is that sprint after sprint after sprint sounds exhausting.

The 30-calendar-day sprint of old has dropped to a common default of two weeks for most Scrum teams. Iterations in other development approaches have also experienced deflation, from months to weeks, from weeks to week and, in many cases, to nothing — the discrete timebox disappearing into a stream of lean continuity. There is no longer a meaningful time- based distinction between sprint and iteration. The remaining distinction is one of context — Scrum vocab or not

— and implication — sprint overwhelmingly suggests speed.

And 'overwhelming' is the problem. Unaware of its origin story and intent, many now favour the word sprint over iteration because of the implication of raw speed, not because they are necessarily employing Scrum. Rather than being shielded from pressures and interruptions,teams routinely experience them with increased frequency and intensity. Rather than finding better ways of working, teams find themselves micromanaged. Rather than being able to manage their flow, teams become overwhelmed.

Which leads us to the seemingly koan-like paradox: sprints are not about sprinting; sprints are about sustainable pace.

Measure for measure

Many teams and managers put a great deal of effort into measuring and tracking their velocity. In theory, what they are tracking is progress over time. In practice, however, they are more likely tracking how much work they have put into developing the
system over a particular period of time, such as a sprint, or how accurate their estimates are, or what their utilisation is.

User stories are often estimated and tracked according to a measure of relative effort, such as story points or T-shirt sizes. The proposed benefit of not using real time is that estimates are decoupled from targets, thus developers should estimate in terms of the functionality rather than being biased by desired dates. Giovanni Asproni[3] highlights the importance of decoupling these concepts:

To be able to estimate well it is obviously important to learn some estimation techniques. First of all, however, it is funda-

---

[3]"LearntoEstimate"byGiovanniAsproni,97ThingsEveryProgrammerShouldKnow, editedbyKevlinHenney.

mental to learn what estimates are, and what they should be used for — as strange as it may seem, many developers and managers don't really know this.

Estimates, targets, and commitments are independent from each other, but targets and commitments should be based on sound estimates.

The intent of story points is to focus on relative sizing independently of other expectations of time. The problem is that, in being numeric, story points become a currency susceptible to arithmetic — especially once they have been aggregated. Rather than the approximation an estimate is intended to be, story points invite conversion while offering the illusion of precision. Once a conversion rate is established, the converted value becomes how people think and talk about them, whether tacitly or explicitly. Story points degenerate into a measure of time, albeit one abstracted enough from real time that, like any currency, they become subject to speculation and inflation. Although a looser fit, T-shirt sizes (S, M, L, XL, etc.) can also fall into the same trap.

And what does the conversion rate — sorry, velocity — mean? If we travel 200 km in two hours, that tells us that we are travelling at 100 km/hour. We have a measure of distance against time. What does it mean to say that a team burned through a total of 100 points in two weeks? If points are a proxy measure of time, we can convert from 100 points to a number of hours or days... which means that the rate derived is a measure of... time against time?! We are either measuring utilisation or we are tracking estimated against actual time, i.e., accuracy of estimation. The one thing we are not measuring is progress in the software developed.

If keeping developers busy was the main goal of software development, all would be good... but the goal of software development lies in the development software, not the consumption of development hours.

As Simon Caulkin notes "The rule is simple: be careful what you measure" by Simon Caulkin[4] :

If there's one management platitude that should have been throttled at birth, it's "what gets measured gets managed". It's not that it's not true — it is — but it is often misunderstood, with disastrous consequences.

The full proposition is: "What gets measured gets managed — even when it's pointless to measure and manage it, and even if it harms the purpose of the organisation to do so."

In case we need [reminding "Principles behind the Agile Manifesto"] (https://agilemanifesto.org/principles.html) :

Working software is the primary measure of progress.

Of course, measuring such progress can be subtle and non-trivial, which is why we often favour simplifications, sometimes at the expense of meaning. As with any abstraction, the problems arise when we fail to understand the limits and implications of our simplifications, and we end up pursuing our abstractions at the expense of our concrete goals, conflating our indications with our ambitions. As H Thomas Johnson cautions:

Perhaps what you measure is what you get. More likely, what you measure is all you'll get. What you don't (or can't) measure is lost.

---

[4]https://theguardian.com/business/2008/feb/10/businesscomment1

The irony of tracking is that it is all too easy to lose track of what we actually want.

The physics of velocity

The language of velocity, which comes originally from Extreme Programming rather than Scrum, is metaphorically compatible with sprint. But there is a subtlety in this word choice that deserves our attention. In everyday language it is common to treat velocity as a synonym of speed, albeit one that sounds more formal and technical. But if we are being formal and technical — a reasonable expectation in the formal and technical discipline of software development — the more precise meaning is that velocity is the rate of change of position, not just the rate of change of distance. To move from one position to another is not just described by a magnitude: it also entails a direction. It is one thing to state we are travelling at 100 km/hour; it is quite another to observe we are travelling 100 km/hour north... especially when we should be heading south.

The busyness of the development team is not that interesting or useful, but it is easy to measure and report. Essentially, this corresponds to speed. The degree to which the team is building the right thing in the right way at a good pace, however, is harder to assess. Harder to assess, but it is meaningful and useful. If you are going to track velocity, then track velocity. Most velocity metrics are actually speed metrics; most speed metrics are just utilisation or estimation metrics. To track velocity, focus on functionality completed (not functionality worked on), focus on functionality delivered (not functionality requested or promised), focus on functionality used (not estimates of business value), track defects (and time spent on defects), track technical debt (not just having it and repaying it, but the consequences of having it[5]) and so on. As in physics, velocity in software development is multidimensional.

If we make speed our focus, we game ourselves to develop faster, which may lead to making ourselves visibly and frantically busy at the expense of meaningful progress. Faster... yet also later and exhausted. Many teams seem to be trapped in a Red Queen's race[6]:

"Well, in our country," said Alice, still panting a little, "you'd generally get to somewhere else—if you ran very fast for a long time, as we've been doing."

"A slow sort of country!" said the Queen. "Now, here, you see, it takes all the running you can do, to keep in the same place. If you want to get somewhere else, you must run at least twice as fast as that!"

Although we may find ourselves nodding along to or advocating the mantra of "deliver better software, faster", we should pause a moment to realise that what we probably mean is "deliver better software, sooner". The difference is both subtle and huge.

The physics of agility

It's not that agility doesn't involve speed; it's more that it involves velocity. But the physics metaphor doesn't stop there. Even understanding progress in terms of direction stops short of fully appreciating that this is not still not what is meant by agile development. Of course, if most teams chasing agility stopped chasing story points and forcing delivery, and

---

[5] "OnExactitudeinTechnicalDebt"byKevlinHenney,oreilly.com/radar/on-exactitude-in-technical-debt
[6] ThroughtheLooking-Glass,andWhatAliceFoundTherebyLewisCarroll

focused instead on identifying and removing obstacles from the path of development, that would be a significant improvement on their status quo. This would definitely be leaner, but it would not necessarily be more agile. It would streamline the flow of development, but it would not necessarily improve the ability to respond to change. For all the non-prescriptiveness of the Agile Manifesto, that is unambiguously a core value:

Responding to change over following a plan

That's what the word agile entails. It is not simply achieving a sustainable speed in an optimal direction; it is being able to change both speed and direction, and to do so easily. It is the second derivative of position with respect to time, not just the first: agility relates both to velocity and to the ability to change it, revising direction and pace as circumstances demand.

The pipeline metaphor often used in software development, from waterfall to CI/CD, can be a helpful starting point, but agility is found not in following the line — or following it at great speed — but in how individuals interact to respond to faults and kinks in the line, to the line veering off, to the line breaking.

Agility is not speed; it's something far more useful and far more interesting.

Kevlin Henney

11. Principles behind the Agile Manifesto

We follow these principles:

Our highest priority is to satisfy the customer through early and continuous delivery of valuable software.

Welcome changing requirements, even late in development. Agile processes harness change for the customer's competitive advantage.

Deliver working software frequently, from a couple of weeks to a couple of months, with a preference to the shorter timescale.

Business people and developers must work together daily throughout the project.

Build projects around motivated individuals. Give them the environment and support they need, and trust them to get the job done.

The most efficient and effective method of conveying information to and within a development team is face-to-face conversation.

Working software is the primary measure of progress.

Agile processes promote sustainable development. The sponsors, developers, and users should be able to maintain a constant pace indefinitely.

Continuous attention to technical excellence and good design enhances agility.

Simplicity–the art of maximizing the amount of work not done–is essential.

The best architectures, requirements, and designs emerge from self-organizing teams.

At regular intervals, the team reflects on how to become more effective, then tunes and adjusts its behaviour accordingly.

12. Standing on the Shoulders of Giants

Just like in every community, all of us are standing on the shoulders of giants. Now we all have our own shoulders we are standing on.Unfortunately our community has lost a few giants.

12.1 Norm Kerth

Norm is the author of Project Retrospectives. If you have ever facilitated a retrospective, you owe him. Unfortunately he was involved in a car accident some years ago and he needs financial help. Although Norm is still alive, we lost him as an active member in our community.

Norm Kerth Support page[1]

12.2 Jean Tabaka

Jean was the author of Collaboration explained. She died in 2016. The friends and colleagues of Jean have created this memorial fund to collect donations in her honor.

Jean Tabaka fund[2]

---

[1]http://www.processimpact.com/norm_kerth.html
[2]http://Www.fund4jean.com

12.3 Mike Beedle

Mike was co-author of the original scrum book. He was an incredible person. Mike was killed by a stranger in 2018. His wife & kids are in need of financial help.

Mike Beedle Support page[3]

12.4 Jerry Weinberg

I know that many people who have contributed to this book have either followed one of Jerry's workshop or have read some of his many books. I think we can't stress enough the influence that Jerry had on the agile community. Alistair Cockburn also told in a talk to celebrate the 20 anniversary speech of Agile Manifesto that they applied techniques they learned from Jerry to facilitate the agile manifesto meeting.

Jerry died 2018/08/07

12.5 David Hussman

David is the inventor of Dude's law. Value is why over how. Where many people & compares focus on the how of agile, when we focus on why we get more results. David wanted to add a piece to this book, yet unfortunately he died before he could finish his advice. Even when David was fighting cancer, I (Yves) felt he was an example on how he dealt with his illness. He died surrounded by the people close to him on 2018/08/19.

---

[3]https://www.gofundme.com/mikebeedlesupport

13. Paying It Forward

A few years ago, I thought the world my kids grow up in, is a much scarier place then the one I grew up in. Today I think that just shows how a privileged person I was growing up.

Working in IT especially as a white men, I live in a privilege world. And I think most of my readers do to.

On this page I want to show a few organisation that can use your help. either money or (better) you help and support. I don't care what organisation you help. I do care you give back and pay it forward.

- Project Alloy[1]

Being the only Latina, the only trans man, or the only disabled person in the room can be tough. Our background should be secondary to our abilities and passions, but we're not there yet. Women, people of color, and other minorities remain dramatically underrepresented in tech. Project Alloy is building a more inclusive technical community, one conference at a time, by offering financial grants and other resources to people who are early in their career and underrepresented in tech.

- CoderDojo[2]

CoderDojo teaches children how to program.

---

[1]https://www.projectalloy.org/
[2]https://www.CoderDojo.com/

- Black Girls Code[3]

To increase the number of women of color in the digital space by empowering girls of color ages 7 to 17 to become innovators in STEM fields, leaders in their communities, and builders of their own futures through exposure to computer science and technology. To provide African-American youth with the skills to occupy some of the 1.4 million computing job openings expected to be available in the U.S. by 2020, and to train 1 million girls by 2040.

- Women who code[4]

We envision a world where women are proportionally represented as technical leaders, executives, founders, VCs, board members, and software engineers.
When you become a part of Women Who Code you gain access to programs and services that are designed to help you step up your tech career. We have over 100,000 members who are career-aged tech professionals operating at each level of the industry.

- Close the gap[5]

Close the Gap is an international non-profit organisation that aims to bridge the digital divide by offering high-quality, pre-owned computers donated by large and medium-sized corporations or public organisations to educational, medical, entrepreneurial and social projects in developing and

[3]http://www.blackgirlscode.com/
[4]https://www.womenwhocode.com/
[5]https://impalabridge.com/

emerging countries. All the projects are demand-driven and share the common denominator of being non-profit-oriented initiatives.

- Impala Bride[6]

Impala Bridge is an Belgian non-profit organisation, also a Tech Network connecting Digital entrepreneurs, Engineers and STEM (Science, Technology, Engineering and mathematics) enthusiasts, with a passion of digital for development.

- Exchange vzw[7]

Growth programmes are always rooted in the local context, by involving relevant South expertise in the programmes. This because on the one hand, the specific local expertise is invaluable, and ensures an in-depth, rich knowledge sharing; on the other hand because it safeguards the knowledge sharing within the local context. This South engagement leads to partnerships with local knowledge centres and local consultants. It goes without saying that, when the expertise is affordably available in that country or a neighbouring country, a South-South collaboration will be established.

Please let me know what other organisations you think I should add.

---

[6]http://close-the-gap.org/
[7]https://exchangevzw.be/

14. Contributors

14.1 Aino Corry

Aino came from a ph.d. in computer science, went back and forth between industry and academia for 10 years until she settled as an independent, where she first and foremost facilitates retrospectives.

Tip: Learning is fun but can be painful

14.2 Allison Pollard

Allison Pollard helps people discover their agile instincts and develop their coaching abilities. As an agile coach with Improving in Dallas, Allison enjoys enabling others to become trusted leaders for change in their organization. In her experience, applying agile methods improves delivery, strengthens relationships, and builds trust between business and IT. Allison is also a Certified Professional Co-Active Coach, a foodie, and proud glasses wearer.

Tip: Becoming Better through the Community

14.3 Angela Riggs

As a QA engineer, Angela believes that empathy and curiosity are driving forces of quality, and uses both to advocate for quality experiences for users and engineering teams. Outside of work, Angela enjoys serious debates about what can truly be categorized as a sandwich. She also has an enthusiasm for karaoke, and once saved the day by knowing every word to No Scrubs.

Tip: Processes should enhance people's ability to work, not prevent it.

14.4 Anke Maerz

My name is Anke Maerz and I have a mission in my life: To see and enjoy beauty in life, and to help other people to see and enjoy it, too.

As a Scrum Master and Agile Coach I live this mission by asking myself every morning THE question: What is it that keeps these amazing people from achieving their goals? – And whatever my answer is, that is where I want to support. Because that is where I can create space for them to see and enjoy the beauty of life.

This has proven very purposeful to me since 2014, when I first got introduced to Agile – and through various big and huge companies in Belgium as well as Germany.

Before getting into Agile I've been project manager and requirements engineer for 2 years, and before that I studied mathematics and psychology at the university of Tübingen (crazy mix? YES! Beautiful, right?!!)

Even before that time I've already been practicing to be a human, which has proven to be most useful on a personal as well as professional level!

Tip: Love is key

14.5 Ardita Karaj

Ardita is a passionate Agile coach, trainer, speaker and consultant in the Toronto area. In her role as President of Industrial Logic Canada she brings more than 15 years of software development experience from different commercial and public organisations. Her focus has been on improvement for organisations that are adopting Agile frameworks. Working across all layers of management and development, she is well known for applying Agile and Lean techniques to help identify and remove barriers to enable the continuous delivery of valuable solutions. She is driven to help companies create sustainable change and has developed techniques that help teams build a culture of continuous improvement.

Tip: Love Your Customer

14.6 Bart Vermijlen

Bart Vermijlen is Co-founder at Box of Birds, a strategic digital design studio based in Antwerp, Belgium. He started his carreer in advertising where he produced multiple award winning campaigns (Cannes Lions, FWA, Awwwards, CCB, LIA,...). He switched to the media sector and became Product Owner at Flemish public broadcaster VRT. in 2018 het co-founded Box of Birds where he combines agile coaching with service and org design. He is Certified Scrummaster (CSM), Certified Agile Leadership (CAL1) and Certified Designthinkers Academy. His passion lies in mixing Agile and Design Thinking into a human-centred cocktail of value driven change.

Tip: Silent Dotvoting

14.7 Ben Linders

Ben Linders is an Independent Consultant in Agile, Lean, Quality, and Continuous Improvement, based in The Netherlands. Author of Getting Value out of Agile Retrospectives, Waardevolle Agile Retrospectives, What Drives Quality and Continuous Improvement. Creator of the Agile Self-assessment Game[1].

Website: BenLinders.com[2]

Tip: Helping team members to solve impediments over solving impediments themselves

14.8 Brenda Bao

I was once a scrum coach who helped big organizations to adopt scrum framework. But those who really adopted it well were those who could think internally from their organizational point of view. Scrum only provides an entry point to start thinking. Based on this observation, I quit the role of scrum coach and started to work with digital projects directly. I find it's much more fun to do the software delivery with the knowledge of agile than talking and coaching agile itself.

Tip: Forget about all the practices and focus on what you deliver

---

[1]https://www.benlinders.com/2016/playing-agile-self-assessment-game/
[2]https://www.benlinders.com/

14.9 Cesario Ramos

Cesario believes that fun, challenge and learning at the work-place is essential for success. He works at large scale transformations worldwide to help create great organization that increase the quality of life for the people, the company and the world. He is also the author of the books Emergent[3] and A Scrum Book[4]. A Certified LeSS Trainer & Professional Scrum Trainer, and frequent conference speaker. In his free time he organises the international Scrum Book Club meetups and the LeSS Recap Days[5].

Tip: Study how the work works

14.10 Chris Matts

An investment banker and agilist who ignored the advise that every ghostbuster's fan knows by heart. He crossed the streams and discovered options that are real. Still a believer in the Agile Manifestio[6], he thinks we should be doing agile and helping others do it rather than simply sell it.

Tip: Happy Storming

---

[3]https://leanpub.com/emergent
[4]http://scrumbook.org/
[5]https://agilix.nl/event/less-practitioner-recap-day/?lang=en
[6]http://agilemanifesto.org/

14.11 Christopher Avery

Christopher Avery, Ph.D., The Responsibility Process[7] guy, authored Teamwork Is An Individual Skill[8] so you can be done with bad teams, and The Responsibility Process so you can unlock and master your natural ability to live and lead with power[9]. He serves The Leadership Gift Program[10] as host and master teacher supporting leaders and coaches pursuing mastery.

or read his longer bio[11]

Tip: Why and How to Claim Wins For Personal and Team Power

14.12 Clare Sudbery

Clare Sudbery is a lead consultant developer with Thoughtworks in the UK[12]. She is an ex high school maths teacher, and is on a mission to help others love their jobs as much as she does. To this end she advocates the following: Embrace learning; Banish intellectual elitism; Provide safe spaces where people can show vulnerability in the workplace; Celebrate diversity in all its forms. She tweets using ClareSudbery[13], and blogs at both a woman in technology[14] and in simple terms[15]

---

[7]https://www.christopheravery.com/responsibility-process
[8]https://www.amazon.com/Teamwork-Individual-Skill-Getting-Responsibility-ebook/dp/B00BYGU8M4
[9]https://www.amazon.com/Responsibility-Process-Unlocking-Natural-Ability-ebook/dp/B01LYB6QV1/
[10]https://www.leadershipgift.com/
[11]http://christopheravery.com/bio
[12]https://www.thoughtworks.com/
[13]https://twitter.com/@ClareSudbery
[14]https://medium.com/a-woman-in-technology
[15]https://insimpleterms.blog/

Tip: Facilitate Learning

14.13 Corey Ladas

Corey Ladas is a pioneer in the field of Lean software development. He created the Scrumban team process and wrote the first book about kanban systems for software development[16]. He currently resides in Portland, Oregon.

Tip: Build Systems, not Software

14.14 Corinna Baldauf

Corinna Baldauf is an agile and lean practitioner from Germany. She is
known for Retromat[17], "24 Work Hacks", and Wall-Skills[18].

Tip Things happen in their own time

14.15 Dana Pylayeva

Dana Pylayeva is an international speaker (50 conferences in 15 countries), trainer,
experienced remote facilitator, the author of several publications and agile games,
including DevOps with Lego and Chocolate[19], Fear in the Workplace[20] and Safety in the Workplace[21].

---

[16]https://www.amazon.com/Scrumban-Essays-Systems-Software-Development-ebook/dp/B004SY63BY

[17]http://Retromat.org

[18]http://Wall-Skills.com

[19]https://www.amazon.com/Introduction-DevOps-Chocolate-LEGO-Scrum-ebook/dp/B01N5SIQQ7

[20]https://www.thegamecrafter.com/games/fear-in-the-workplace

[21]https://www.thegamecrafter.com/games/safety-in-the-workplace

She draws her inspiration from the 20+ years of hands-on experience in IT, Business Agility/ DevOps culture coaching, working with international clients and facilitating change in Fortune 500 companies.

Dana is a certified Training from the Back of the Room trainer, Open
Space facilitator, CSM, CSP, CSPO, and Certified LeSS Practitioner.
She is the founder of the Big Apple Scrum Day conference in NYC and a
leader of NYC Liberating Structures community.

Tip: Every team needs a Working Agreement

14.16 Dan Terhorst-North

Daniel Terhorst-North uses his deep technical and operational knowledge to help business and technology leaders to optimise digital product organisations. He puts people first and finds simple, pragmatic solutions to business and technical problems, often using lean and agile techniques. With thirty years of experience in IT, Daniel is a frequent speaker at technology and business conferences worldwide. The originator of Behaviour-Driven Development (BDD) and Deliberate Discovery, Daniel has published feature articles in numerous software and business publications, and contributed to The RSpec Book: Behaviour Driven Development with RSpec, Cucumber, and Friends and 97 Things Every Programmer Should Know: Collective Wisdom from the Experts. He occasionally blogs at https://dannorth.net/blog[22].

Tip: Working Software Over Comprehensive Documentation

---
[22]https://dannorth.net/blog

14.17 Daria Bagina

Daria is a Professional Scrum Trainer and a practicing Scrum Master. Her focus is to help teams and organizations to create better working environments. The kind of workplaces where self-organizing self-motivated teams build awesome products.

One of her strengths is creativity. Thanks to the creative approach teams she works with discover new ways to look at old problems and find new solutions. She adapts her teachings and practices to each situation she encounters to increase engagement and empower people to make decisions.

Tip: Don't forget to mine for conflict

14.18 David (dude) Hussman

If you don't know where you are going, it's easy to iteratively not get there."
David Hussman was a thundering catalyst and pioneer for the agile community.
Unfortunately he died before he could finish his tip.

14.19 Deepti Jain

Deepti has a reputation for her innovative power with which she strategies various learning and networking 'Experiences' for her clients and community to Build Agile Capability and to achieve Sustainable Transformation resulting in continuous growth.

To get access and share Agile abundance she founded "Agile-Virgin[23] - An Agility Solutioning Boutique" in 2015. In addition to Agile Consulting, Coaching, and Training, AgileVirgin also runs a Countrywide Community of Practices, connecting Agilists across India and bridging them to Global Lean Agile Change Agents. She loves to connect and collaborate and prefers to call herself a Social Scientist, always feeling herself where technology meets people.

Here are international unconferences, forums and experiences that Deepti crafted - AgilityToday, Agile-A-Thon, Funconf, Change Agents Summit, Elucidate, Agile Coach Camp, Agile Career Bootcamp, Narrathon, Agile Job fair and Women-in-Agile-and-Tech. Furthermore, Women in Agile and Tech runs Global Mentorship Program, Dream Big, Visuallect, Gamify it, Unleash Yourself and Agility A2Z.

She also worked with Agile Alliance[24] as Initiative Director for Building Future Leaders and Change Agents[25], and India Community Development Chief to help India meet the need to grow Lean-Agile Leaders and Change Agents who can shape the culture of the country and help its industries achieve a true Agile Mindset.

You can connect with her over one of the following channels:
Email[26]
LinkedIn[27]
Twitter[28]

Tip: Fool didn't know it was impossible, so she did it!

---

[23]https://www.agilevirgin.in/
[24]https://www.agilealliance.org
[25]https://www.agilealliance.org/resources/initiatives/building-future-leaders-and-change-agents/
[26]deepti.jain@agilealliance.org
[27]https://www.linkedin.com/in/dee-j/
[28]https://twitter.com/agilevirgin

14.20 Diana Larsen

Visionary pragmatist, Diana Larsen, is co-founder, Chief Connector and a principal coach, consultant, and mentor at the Agile Fluency® Project, based in Portland OR, USA.

As contributions to the Agile community, Diana co-authored the books Agile Retrospectives: Making Good Teams Great; Liftoff: Start and Sustain Successful Agile Teams; Five Rules for Accelerated Learning. She co-originated the Agile Fluency® model and co-authored the eBook, The Agile Fluency Model: A Brief Guide to Success with Agile. For 25+ years, she led the practice area for Agile software development, leading & managing teams, and guiding Agile transitions at FutureWorks Consulting. She delivers keynote talks at conferences around the world, participates in podcast interviews, and speaks at local and regional agile groups, as her schedule allows.

Since 2015 she has devoted her energy to a new endeavor. Through the Agile Fluency Project's programs for training, mentoring, and supporting agile coaches and consultants, Diana shares the wisdom she's gained in over 30 years of working with leaders, teams, and organizations.

To serve her communities, Diana facilitates productive Open Space Technology events and delivers inspiring conference keynote talks around the world.

Tip: Become a continuous learner

14.21 Emilie Franchomme

Emilie joined the french Agile Community in 2007. She started as a Product Owner and later became a Scrum Master. She enjoys meeting with peers and sharing knowledge and stories at meetups and conferences. She is a co-chair for Big Apple Scrum Day[29] conference in New York, where she moved in 2014.

Tip: Care about feedback

14.22 Emily Webber

Emily Webber is a London-based independent Agile and digital delivery consultant, coach, trainer and speaker. Her focus is on how people work together, giving people the skills they need and creating the right environment for awesome delivery.

She helps those going through digital transformations develop their capability for sustainable change.

She was the head of agile delivery at the Government Digital Service, where she built, developed and led a team of about 40 agile delivery professionals. At GDS, she created the widely-followed approach and maturity model for communities of practice, and subsequently authored Building Successful Communities of Practice.

Emily is a popular keynote speaker, blogger[30] and event organiser. She has spoken at Mind the Product London, GOTO Copenhagen and Craft. Emily set up Agile in Leeds, Agile

---

[29]https://www.bigapplescrumday.org/
[30]https://emilywebber.co.uk

on the Bench[31], and Agile in the Ether[32], among others. Her experiences on the event circuit prompted her to create the Diversity Charter[33].

Tip: Support the interactions between individuals

14.23 George Dinwiddie

George Dinwiddie helps organizations develop software more effectively.
He brings decades of development experience from electronic hardware and embedded firmware to business information technology. He helps organizations, managers, and teams solve the problems they face by providing consulting, coaching, mentoring and training at the
organizational, process, team, interpersonal, and technical levels.
Involved in the Agile community since 2000, he has helped groups ranging from a 6-person startup to a Fortune 100 company and a billion-plus dollar federal program, either directly or in partnership with other companies. He is the author of Evolutionary Anatomy of Test Automation Code[34], co-author of Patterns of Agile Journeys[35], he also wrote Software Estimation without guessing[36]

The promoter of the "Three Amigos" name for collaborative exploration of business requirements, George has worked with others to further the practical application of Behavior

---

[31]http://agileonthebench.co.uk/

[32]http://agileintheether.co.uk/

[33]https://diversitycharter.org/

[34]https://leanpub.com/EvolutionaryAnatomy

[35]https://leanpub.com/agilejourneys

[36]https://pragprog.com/titles/gdestimate/software-estimation-without-guessing/

Driven Development (BDD). He helps organizations refine their business requirements to produce long-term documentation and automated verification in the process.

Tip: Bypassing Binary Thinking for Better Understanding

14.24 Heidi Helfand

Heidi Helfand[37] is author of the book Dynamic Reteaming[38]. She coaches fast-growing companies using practical, people-focused techniques. At ExpertCity, Inc. (acquired by Citrix) she was on the development team that invented GoToMyPC, GoToMeeting and GoToWebinar. Then she was Principal Agile Coach at AppFolio, Inc. makers of workflow software for property management and law verticals where she built a coaching group to support dynamic, cross-functional teams. She is currently at Procore Technologies – a leading provider of cloud-based applications for construction. At Procore[39], Heidi is in R&D leadership, coaching on software development and reteaming best practices.

Tip: Empower "Team Change"

14.25 Henrik Kniberg

Henrik Kniberg is an organizational consultant at Crisp[40] in Stockholm. He has spent the past few years working primarily with Lego and Spotify. He enjoys helping companies succeed with both the technical and human sides of product

---

[37]https://www.heidihelfand.com/
[38]https://www.heidihelfand.com/dynamic-reteaming/
[39]https://www.procore.com/
[40]https://www.crisp.se/

development using agile and lean principles, as described in his popular books Scrum and XP from the Trenches[41] and Kanban and Scrum, making the most of both[42] and Lean from the Trenches[43], as well as his viral videos Agile Product Ownership in a Nutshell[44] and Spotify Engineering Culture[45]. Henrik has recently become engaged in climate change, he created the video Friendly Guide to Climate Change[46] and is involved with GoClimateNeutral[47], Trine[48], and other startups in that space.

Tip: Observe

14.26 Hina Popal

Hina[49] is an Agile Practitioner at Red Hat[50]. Before Red Hat, Hina was doing government contracting work while pursuing her passion for Agile avoiding process related bottlenecks. She is always on the quest for creating great team environments and drinking great cups of coffee and tea.

Tip: Eliminate comparison and encourage progres

---

[41]https://www.infoq.com/minibooks/scrum-xp-from-the-trenches-2
[42]https://www.infoq.com/minibooks/kanban-scrum-minibook
[43]https://pragprog.com/book/hklean/lean-from-the-trenches
[44]http://blog.crisp.se/2012/10/25/henrikkniberg/agile-product-ownership-in-a-nutshell
[45]https://labs.spotify.com/2014/03/27/spotify-engineering-culture-part-1/
[46]https://www.youtube.com/watch?v=3CM_KkDuzGQ
[47]https://www.goclimateneutral.org/
[48]https://www.jointrine.com/
[49]https://twitter.com/hi_popal
[50]https://www.redhat.com/en

14.27 Ilan Kirschenbaum

Ilan fell in love with computer programming at the age of
13. He became a professional programmer in 1987, developing
software in various roles, from coding and testing to product
management and architecture. After attending a Groups Re-
lations workshop in 2002, the seeds were planted for his new
love: developing teams and organizations. When Ilan met the
agile movement he decided to re-route this passion as his new
career path. Since then Ilan has devoted himself to helping
individuals, teams and organizations, and to deepen his learning in organizational development, facilitation, engineering
excellence, (de-)scaling organizations and basically anything
related to agile organizations.

Tip: The value of reverie

14.28 Irene Kuhn

Irene is a Scrum Master with a passion for coaching. Coming
from an IT background she easily gets in touch with teams
where her main focus is providing just enough structure
so that they can grow into confident, self-organizing teams
while teaching them the skills to get there. She's helping
organisations find their way to agility with curiosity, listening
and patience as her companions.

Tip: Holding Space for growth

14.29 Ivan Darmawan

Ivan has been 20 years since starting his journey in software development. He thought that the business environment complexity has been increasing rapidly. Many knowledges have been obsolete almost in no time. So the business agility way of working with Scrum is his favorite strategy that he needs to embrace to face upcoming complexity and uncertainty. As business agility is more and more being embraced by many companies, he and his partners are encouraged to initiate a company Adaptiva.co.id to help those companies in implementing business agility. On social media, you can find him at linkedin[51] or Facebook[52].

Tip: RI Mode Sprint Planning

14.30 Ivo Peksens

I am an Influencer, Change agent, Scrum Master and Agile Coach. I value curiosity, respect and trust. I help individuals and organisations understand the Agile mindset and make use of it in practice.

Since 2013, actively growing theoretically and practically in Lean, Kanban, Scrum and Agile. I have been contributing in local and international organizations as a Scrum Master and Agile Coach. I have been building relationships and learnt from coaches and mentors beyond Latvia, organising/co-creating events in Latvia and co-creating annual Agile Lean Europe (ALE) unconference since 2015.

---

[51]https://linkedin.com/in/ivandarmawan
[52]https://facebook.com/ivan.darmawan

My goal in Latvia is to promote and develop the Agile Coaching profession. If you are interested, please join the Agile Coaching Latvia facebook group[53]

Tip: Increase quality of meetings

14.31 Jeff Patton

Jeff Patton helps companies adopt a way of working that's focused on building great products, not just building stuff faster. Jeff blends a mixture of Agile thinking, Lean and Lean Startup Thinking, and UX Design and Design Thinking to end up with a holistic product-centric way of working. Jeff is author of the bestselling O'Reilly book User Story Mapping which describes a simple holistic approach to using stories in Agile development without losing sight of the big picture. You can learn more about Jeff at: jpattonassociates.com.

Tip: 9 Rules of thumb to improve your backlog refinement workshops

14.32 Jenni Jepsen

Jenni Jepsen[54] helps people transform organizations to create lasting change. By focusing on the value to be achieved and understanding where clients are at and where they want to go, Jenni works closely with them to increase organizational effectiveness, motivation and results. Jenni is an expert in change leadership and communications, and integrates neuroscience and Intent-based Leadership concepts into her

---

[53] https://www.facebook.com/groups/agilecoachinglatvia
[54] https://goagile.dk/

coaching, training and sparring with leaders at every level. Jenni consults, writes and speaks worldwide about leadership, teams, and how to take advantage of how our brains function to get optimal thinking in the workplace.

Tip: Stop protecting your team

14.33 Jerry Weinberg

Jerry's always been interested in helping smart people be happy and productive. To that end, he's published more than 60 award-winning best-selling non-fiction books on human behavior, thinking, leadership, and all phases of information technology. He incorporates his knowledge of science, engineering, and human behavior into all of his writing, including mysteries, science fiction, and technothrillers about smart people. Jerry is a charter member in the Computing Hall of Fame, but the "award" he's most proud of is the book, The Gift of Time (Fiona Charles, ed.) written by his students and fans for his 75th birthday. These stories show he's been quite successful at helping smart people be happy.

Jerry died while this book was collected.

Foreword

14.34 Jimmy Janlén

Jimmy Janlén is an agile coach and teacher at Crisp (Stockholm). In addition to coaching, Jimmy holds courses, writes books, blogs and creates videos on all things agile and lean such as agile leadership, agile adaptations, large scale agile, team dynamics and facilitation. He sometimes refers to himself as a bureaucracy therapist, cultural acupuncture, cross company pollinator and visualization magician. Jimmy is the author of the book Visualization Examples[55], available on Amazon on LeanPub.

Tip: Visualize More!

14.35 Joanne Perold

Joanne has worked in the software industry since 2003 in roles ranging from product management to writing functions and creating business intelligence. In 2009 she went on her first Scrum course and discovered the world of Agile and a different approach to developing software. Since then she has worked with teams and organisations to transform and improve the way they work. Through these interactions she has worked with many contexts and different ways to apply Agile principles. Joanne is passionate about learning and growing both herself and her teams. This curiosity led her to the AYE (Amplify your Effectiveness) conference, the PSL (Problem Solving Leadership) course with Jerry Weinberg, and Dave Snowden's Cynefin training. Attending these conferences and courses not only connected her to the international community but helped her to grow as a coach, a leader, a mentor, a problem solver and a critical thinker.

Tip: Crafting Quality Interactions

---

[55]https://leanpub.com/agiletoolbox-visualizationexamples

14.36 Johanna Rothman

Johanna Rothman, known as the "Pragmatic Manager," provides frank advice for your tough problems. She helps leaders and teams see problems, resolve risks, and manage their product development.

Johanna[56] was the Agile 2009 conference chair and was the co-chair of the first edition of the Agile Practice Guide. Johanna is the author of more then fourteen books[57], including Create Your Successful Agile Project[58], Agile and Lean Program Management[59], and Manage Your Project Portfolio[60]. She is working on books about geographically distributed teams, product ownership, and management.

Tip: Know The Work

14.37 Judy Rees

Judy Rees, creator of the ENGAGE model for remote facilitation, has introduced scores of trainers, coaches and facilitators to the joy of live online training – including within large organisations such as the RSA[61]. For the last three years she's been the host of one of the world's first online-video un-conferences, Metaphorum, which connects 150 people around the world in a 13-hour live-learning marathon. She's the co-author of Clean Language: Revealing Metaphors And Open-

---

[56]https://www.jrothman.com/
[57]https://www.jrothman.com/books/
[58]https://www.jrothman.com/books/#CYSAP
[59]https://www.jrothman.com/books/#ALPM
[60]https://www.jrothman.com/books/#MYPP
[61]https://www.thersa.org/

ing Minds[62] and is a regular keynote speaker at Agile and other events around the world.

Tip: How To Reduce Groupthink In remote Meetings

14.38 Jürgen De Smet

Jurgen is a Certified LeSS (Large-Scale Scrum) Trainer, his engagements with clients achieve greater organisational alignment with fewer dependencies left to manage. Transparency with access to good data ensures empirical-sound decision making. As a result, the system becomes leaner, more customer-centric and ready with each successive change wave to build its greatest products yet. Inside he is still skateboarding, picking up new moves, adapting to ever-changing environments and freestyling with the best, wherever fresh design concepts for improving the world of work are emerging and being perfected.

Tip: The gut feeling ordering practice

14.39 Jutta Eckstein

Jutta works as an independent coach, consultant, trainer, author, and speaker. She has helped many teams and organizations worldwide to make an agile transition. She has a unique experience in applying agile processes within medium-sized to large distributed mission-critical projects. She has published her experience in her books. She is the co-author of 'Company-wide Agility with Beyond Budgeting, Open Space

---

[62]https://www.amazon.com/Clean-Language-Revealing-Metaphors-Opening/dp/1845901258/

& Sociocracy' and 'Diving for Hidden Treasures: Uncovering the Cost of Delay in your Project Portfolio'. She is the author of 'Agile Software Development in the Large', 'Agile Software Development with Distributed Teams', and 'Retrospectives for Organizational Change'.

She is a member of the Agile Alliance (having served the board of directors from 2003-2007) and a member of the program committee of many different American, Asian, and European conferences, where she has also presented her work.

Tip: Are You Really Doing It?

14.40 Kanatcha Sakdiset

Kanatcha is an agile coach and consultant from Thailand but now based in Naarm (Melbourne), Australia.

Kanatcha helps teams and organisations transition towards the happier and more sustainable ways of working. She believes it's more important to change systemically rather than individually.

Kanatcha enjoys riding her bike by the Birrarung river and taking pictures of food before she eats it.

Tip: Montague Street Bridge

14.41 Karen Catlin

Karen Catlin is a leadership coach and an acclaimed author and speaker on inclusive workplaces. After spending twenty-five years building software products and serving as a vice president of engineering at Macromedia and Adobe, she witnessed a sharp decline in the number of women working in tech. Frustrated but galvanized, she knew it was time to switch gears.

Today, Karen coaches women to be stronger leaders and men to be better allies for members of all underrepresented groups. Her client roster includes Airbnb, DoorDash, eBay, Envoy, Intel, Intuit, and Segment, as well as entrepreneurs and individuals. Karen's coaching offerings include tactics for increasing visibility, being more strategic, managing stake-holders, negotiation, and cultivating ally skills. Her writing on these and related topics has appeared in Inc., the Daily Beast, Fast Company, and the Muse, and she's consulted on articles for the Wall Street Journal, Forbes, and the New York Times.

To help more people cultivate ally skills, Karen wrote Better Allies: Everyday Actions to Create Inclusive, Engaging Workplaces[63]. She also published a companion guidebook, The Better Allies™ Approach to Hiring, with best practices to recruit and hire people from underrepresented groups. In 2020, her unique approach to allyship was featured in the BBC's Ally Track tool[64].

Karen Catlin speaking at the University of Nebraska Women in Tech Summit 2016A self-professed public speaking geek, Karen is a highly sought-after and engaging presenter who has delivered talks at hundreds of conferences and corporate events. She speaks on inclusive workplaces and women in leadership. Her TEDx talk, Women in Tech: The Missing Force[65], explores the decline in gender diversity in tech, why it's a problem, and what can be done about it. In addition to

---

[63]https://betterallies.com/
[64]https://www.bbc.co.uk/creativediversity/allyshipapp/#/
[65]https://www.youtube.com/watch?v=8uiEHaDSfgI

speaking herself, Karen is determined to change the ratio for who is on stage giving keynotes and other presentations. To support this goal, she coauthored Present! A Techie's Guide to Public Speaking[66] with Poornima Vijayashanker[67].

Karen is a graduate and active alum of Brown University, serving as an advisor to the university's Computer Science Diversity Initiative and mentoring students on how to launch their careers. She's also a member of the board of directors of Digital NEST and on the advisory boards for the Women's CLUB of Silicon Valley and WEST (Women Entering & Staying in Technology). In 2015, the California State Assembly honored Karen with the Wonder Women Tech Innovator Award for outstanding achievements in business and technology and for being a role model for women.

Are you looking for a leadership coach who understands what it takes to be successful as a woman in Silicon Valley? Are you a leader who wants to create a more inclusive workplace? Are you seeking an inspirational speaker for your next event? Contact Karen[68]. She looks forward to hearing from you.

Tip: Let's talk about the p-word

14.42 Karen Graeves

Karen is a co-founder of Growing Agile and an Agile Coach at ANZ.

She enjoys helping people bring joy and balance back into their work lives. A firm believer in having fun at work because it makes her happier and more productive.

---

[66]https://www.amazon.com/gp/product/1535403756/
[67]https://www.amazon.com/Poornima-Vijayashanker/e/B00STO0F4U/
[68]https://karencatlin.com/contact/

When she's not working, she enjoys trail running, travelling, eating good food and wine, and spending time relaxing at home with her husband, cats and her xbox.

Tip: Arrive with your whole heart

14.43 Karthik Kamal Balasubramaniam

Karthik is an Agile Coach/Consultant with AgileFAQs[69]. He is passionate about coaching teams and organisation in Agile/Lean ways of working. Have coached teams in Intel, S&P, ING, HCL, Hike etc. He also specialises in psychology and product management. Besides coaching teams he also runs dialogue based events in Bangalore, which focuses on normalising therapeutic conversations.

Tip: Question Your Teams Intimacy

14.44 Katrina Clokie

Katrina Clokie is a General Manager of Engineering at Xero. Katrina is seen as a leader in the international testing community as the author of A Practical Guide to Testing in DevOps[70], an international keynote speaker[71], a co-founder of the WeTest New Zealand testing community that is now known as Ministry of Testing NZ, the founder of Testing Trapeze magazine,

---

[69]https://agilefaqs.com/
[70]http://katrinatester.blogspot.com/p/testing-in-devops.html
[71]http://katrinatester.blogspot.com/p/speaking-engagements.html

blogger and tweeter[72]. Her complete professional profile is available on LinkedIn[73].

Tip: Different Ideas for Defect Management

14.45 Kevlin Henney

Kevlin Henney is an independent consultant, trainer, reviewer and writer. His development interests, contributions and work with companies covers programming, people and practice. He has been a columnist for various magazines and web sites, a contributor to open- and closed-source software and a member of more committees than is probably healthy (it has been said that "a committee is a cul-de-sac down which ideas are lured and then quietly strangled"). He is co-author of two volumes in the Pattern-Oriented Software Architecture series, editor of 97 Things Every Programmer Should Know and co-editor of 97 Things Every Java Programmer Should Know.

Tip: agile =/= Speed

14.46 Lanette Creamer

Lanette Creamer has loved technology since she got online on the family Commodore 64 to play Telearena with friends on a Major BBS. Born and raised in the Pacific Northwest near Seattle, I love my home town and plan to stay here long term. A cat lady at the core, she loves purring creatures who are uncooperative at times, which explains her enjoying programing and herding cats. As a technical program manager, her main

---

[72]https://twitter.com/katrinaclokie
[73]https://www.linkedin.com/in/katrina-clokie-37041211a/?originalSubdomain=nz

focus is on serving happy customers, advocating for happy developers and informing stakeholders. All truths pair better with sincerity and candor.

Tip: Building client trust

14.47 Linda Rising

Linda Rising is an independent consultant who lives near Nashville, Tennessee. Linda has a Ph.D. from Arizona State University in object-based design metrics. Her background includes university teaching as well as work in industry in telecommunications, avionics, and tactical weapons systems. She is an internationally known presenter on topics related to agile development, patterns, retrospectives, the change process, and the connection between the latest neuroscience and software development. Linda is the author of numerous articles and several books. The latest, More Fearless Change, co-authored with Mary Lynn Manns. Her web site is: www.lindarising.org[74]

Tip: The evolutionary path from authority to agility

14.48 Lisa Crispin

Lisa Crispin is the co-author, with Janet Gregory, of three books: Agile Testing
Condensed: A Brief Introduction, More Agile Testing: Learning Journeys for the Whole
Team, Agile Testing: A Practical Guide for Testers and Agile Teams; the LiveLessons

---

[74]http://www.lindarising.org

Agile Testing Essentials video course, and "The Whole Team Approach to Agile
Testing" 3-day training course offered through the Agile Testing Fellowship. Lisa was
voted by her peers as the Most Influential Agile Testing Professional Person at Agile
Testing Days in 2012. She is a testing advocate working at mabl to explore leading
practices in testing in the software community. Please visit lisacrispin.com[75] and agiletester[76] for more.

Tip: Retrospectives are the most valuable agile practice

14.49 Lisette Sutherland

Lisette Sutherland is a remote-working German-born American living in the Netherlands who is totally jazzed by the fact that it's possible to work from anywhere. In fact, it's not just possible; it's completely, productively workable – if you do it right. Her company, Collaboration Superpowers[77], shares just how to do it right in a variety of formats:

- Work Together Anywhere Handbook coverWork Together Anywhere: A Handbook on Working Remotely — Successfully — for Individuals, Teams, and Managers
- Speaking engagements and webinars

Work Together Anywhere workshops

---

[75]www.lisacrispin.com
[76]www.agiletester.ca
[77]https://www.collaborationsuperpowers.com/

- Weekly podcasts featuring interviews with remote-working experts
- Bi-monthly newsletter
- Guest appearances at Pilar Orti's 21st-Century Work Life podcasts

Tip: Create a high-bandwidth work environment

14.50 Madhavi Ledalla

Madhavi is a transformational enthusiast with technology back ground and end-to-end development experience with MS technologies.

She has keen interest in delivering customised workshops that include User Story, Product Owner, Scrum Master, Design Thinking, Release Planning & Portfolio workshops. She works with leadership & teams to guide them through transformation.

Her practices include training and coaching in varied Agile methods including Scrum and Kanban and Scaling frameworks such as SAFe and LeSS.

Madhavi played multiple roles of Scrum Master, Coach, Project Manager and a Technologist. This has given her the ability to understand team dynamics to navigate transformational challenges.

Madhavi is a Speaker, Reviewer & Organizer for Regional/-Global Agile conferences

Tip: Self-organizing teams

14.51 Michael Sahota

Michael K Sahota, Certified Enterprise Coach, Trainer, Consultant, Culture and Leadership Expert. Michael teaches his proven framework for leading successful Agile Transformations in his highly accoladed Certified Agile Leadership (CAL 1 & 2) Training worldwide. As a thought leader, in 2012, he published the ground-breaking book "An Agile Adoption and Transformation Survival Guide: Working with Organizational Culture". In 2017 alone, he has trained over 600 Agile leaders worldwide, giving them the internal growth, knowledge and skills needed to deliver high performance organizations.

Tip: Ask for permission

14.52 Mina Boström Nakicenovic

Mina is a passionate IT leader with 20+ years of experience in software development. She worked as a developer, software architect, development manager and now she works as a Head of Development. Apart from Mina's big passion for technology, she developed also a big interest for innovation management and leadership questions. Mina's passion for software development has spread within her family. She and her husband Gustav are often taking their three kids to conferences, where they are presenting together as an agile family.

Tip: You are an informal leader – which leadership skills do you need?

14.53 Michele Sliger

Michele Sliger has worked in software development for 30 years, and has been
embracing change with agile methodologies for the last 20 of those years. Co-author of
the book The Software Project Manager's Bridge to Agility and a self-described "bridge
builder," her passion lies in helping those in traditional software development
environments cross the bridge to agility. Sliger is the owner of Sliger Solutions Inc.,
where she consults to businesses ranging from small start-ups to Fortune 500 companies,
helping teams with their agile adoption and helping organizations prepare for the changes
that agile adoption brings. Michele holds PMP ® and PMI-ACP ® credentials from the
Project Management Institute, is a Certified Scrum Trainer (CST), and has an
undergraduate MIS degree and an MBA. She can be reached at michele@sligersolutions.com

Tip: Becoming Comfortable with Being Uncomfortable

14.54 Michael Hill

GeePaw Hill is a coach – a professional harvester of the value of change – in the software development industry. A geek for forty years, he's spent the last two decades helping individuals, teams, and organizations take steps to become closer to who or how they wish to be. You can reach him through his site[78]:

Tip: Craft Experiences Not Arguments

14.55 Mike Cohn

Mike Cohn helps organizations and individuals succeed with agile. With more than 20 years of agile experience, Mike has previously been a technology executive in companies of various sizes, from startup to Fortune 40. He is the author of Agile Estimating and Planning, User Stories Applied for Agile Software Development, and Succeeding with Agile. His weekly email tips are enjoyed by more than 100,000 subscribers. He can be reached at mike@mountaingoatsoftware.com[79] or through Mountain Goat Software[80]

Tip: The scrum police are coming for you (or are they?)

14.56 Molood Ceccarelli

Molood Ceccarelli is a remote work strategist and agile coach. She is often referred to as the queen of remote work in agile circles. She is the founder of Remote Forever Summit, an annual online summit about distributed agile that has been around since 2016 and has attracted over 10k attendees from around the world. Her company Remote Forever helps distributed companies adopt agile ways of working and helps agile companies work remotely effectively. Her work has

---

[78]https://geepawhill.org
[79]email:mike@mountaingoatsoftware.com
[80]https://www.mountaingoatsoftware.com

been published in places such as Forbes, Huffington Post and Inc.com as well as Scrum Alliance.

Tip: Asynchronous management: Simplicity in a digital workplace

14.57 Nadezhda Belousova

Nadezhda is a Founder of Evolneo GmbH a management consulting company with the purpose to inspire and enable conscious organisational evolution through the lens of living systems. She is an Enterprise Business Agility Strategist and an integral value catalyst who deeply cares about high-performing scalable businesses with human-centric approach and sustainability at heart. She brings a combination of psychology, multiple professional coaching approaches (the Integral Method™, ORSC, Solution-Focused coaching, Clean Language, etc.), extensive hands-on consulting experience in various industries, and a can-do-all mindset. Nadezhda is an active member of business agility and organisational development communities where she cross-pollinates and synthesises ideas across domains, and accelerates agility in the business ecosystems.

Tip: Agile Coaching Agreement as Creative Partnership

14.58 Naresh Jain, Founder ConfEngine

Developer... Consultant... Conference Producer... Startup Founder... Struggling to stay up-to-date with technology innovation.

Null Process Evangelist. Naresh Jain is an internationally recognized Technology & Product Development Expert. Over the last decade, he has helped streamline the product development culture at many Fortune 500 companies like Google, Amazon, HP, Siemens Medical, GE Energy, Schlumberger, EMC, CA Technologies, to name a few. His hands-on approach to product innovation by focusing on product discovery and engineering excellence is a key differentiator. Naresh founded the Agile Software community of India and organises the Agile India conference. He is also responsible for organising 50+ international conferences including the Functional Conf, Simple Design & Testing Conference, Agile Coach Camp, Selenium Conf India, jQuery/Open Web Conference, Open Data Science Conf India and Eclipse Summit India. In recognition of his accomplishments, in 2007 the Agile Alliance awarded Naresh with the Gordon Pask Award[81] for contributions to the Agile Community.

Tip: You will never arrive at THE destination

14.59 Nele Van Beveren

Tip: Since all those companies work Agile, we don't longer receive any commitment

14.60 Nicole Belilos

Nicole Belilos is an experienced Agile coach and Scrum Trainer (CST). She helps organizations, teams and individuals on their journey to Agility

---

[81]https://www.infoq.com/news/2007/08/2007-pask-awards

Nicole has a background in Mathematics and Computer Science. She started her career as a programmer in the waterfall world. In 2004, she was introduced to Scrum and the Agile community. From then on, she has been an enthusiastic adept of Agile.

As a trainer, speaker and event organizer, Nicole is strongly involved in the Agile community For more details, visit her website[82]

Nicole is also the co-founder of the Dutch YouTube channel: from A to agile[83]

Tip: Be like a good parent

14.61 Oana Juncu

Oana likes to call herself an Agile Business DJ mixing whatever practices inspired from various domains like system thinking to UX and neurosciences, will help people and organisations become proud of their outcomes. She builds shared leadership programs that work to creating awareness on collective fears so they can turn into an ally that can help transformation programs succeed.

Tip: Ownership in Agile: Purpose and collaboration

14.62 Olaf Lewitz

Trust Artist and Leadership Coach from Berlin.
"Coaching is life-changing. If it is not life-changing, it is not

---

[82]www.nicolebelilos.com
[83]https://www.youtube.com/channel/UCTRX9fTkgJUvp9CEFHGnDCQ

coaching."

After 20+ years of working, leading, rebelling, soothing, coaching and playing in corporations of all sizes and flavours he's found his passion: To increase people's level of awareness around liberation. To help people see where we have choices: to be invited, to invite, to be free.

His motto is: "You deserve to love what you do."

Tip: Effective Teams Are NOT Efficient

14.63 Ole Jepsen

Ole Jepsen is a transformation advisor at Denmark-based goAgile, working with organizations looking to lead change. Using his expertise in Agile methodologies, Intent-based Leadership and facilitation, Ole works with companies and leaders to create workplaces where people thrive and deliver value. Ole is a founder of the Agile Leadership Network and numerous Denmark-based Agile groups, and is active in the international Agile community, speaking at conferences and consulting worldwide.

Tip: Stop protecting your team

14.64 Phil Gadzinski

Phil holds deeply that agility requires a human centred, system wide approach where the ultimate goal is to make work better for people. To do this you need to understand why and how work happens in an organisation and plan, contextually, on how to enable leaders to create the space for people to work differently. My passion is helping people realise change starts with them and giving them the advice and support needed to make it happen at scale with a nudge here, a wink there.

My focus is large enterprises who can see and feel the promise of agility, and need the confidence to change the status quo

Tip: where did governance go

14.65 Rashina Hoda

Dr Rashina Hoda is a senior lecturer in software engineering at the University of Auckland, New Zealand. Rashina's research and teaching practice has focused on agile and lean software development for over a decade. She has written on a variety of agile topics, including an award-winning theory of becoming agile (ICSE 2017) and a review of the rise and evolution of agile in the IEEE software's 50th anniversary of software engineering special issue. She enjoys presenting the 'voice of agile research' to practitioners and academics alike. For more information, see www.rashina.com

Tip: Enable Growth

14.66 Ravi Kumar

Change agent & hands-on practitioner enabling organization change and IT delivery excellence by challenging the status quo and leveraging subject matter expertise in implementing agile/lean software processand practices. Agile is a philosophy to me much more than a software methodology or framework. I work with the leadership, management and development teams to create enterprise agile transformation roadmap, strategy, culture change and sustainable agile practice. I am an invited speaker at conferences and local community meet up events, conference chair and program committee member at Agile India[84] and a founding member of Agile Leadership Network - Bengaluru Chapter.

Tip: Coaching teams: A journey of contradictions and context as a crucial driver

14.67 Rini Vansolingen

Rini van Solingen[85] is a speaker, author, professor, and entrepreneur. Every year he gives more than 150 lectures about speed and agility of people and organizations. Rini is a part-time full professor at Delft University of Technology and he is also CTO at Prowareness We-On. Rini is the author of a number of management books, including The Power of Scrum[86] (2011 - with Jeff Sutherland and Eelco Rustenburg), Scrum for Managers[87] (2015 – with Rob van Lanen), the management novel: How to lead self-managing teams?[88] (2016), and Formula-X: how to bring extreme acceleration in organizations[89] (2020 - with Jurriaan Kamer).

Tip: Never forget that Scrum is just as simple as chess!

---

[84]https://2020.agileindia.org/

[85]http://www.rinivansolingen.com

[86]https://www.amazon.com/Power-Scrum-Jeff-Sutherland-ebook/dp/B007474YMC

[87]https://www.amazon.com/Scrum-Managers-Management-Results-Driven-Organizations/dp/0990466523

[88]https://www.amazon.com/How-Lead-Self-Managing-Teams-sheepherding/dp/153763903X/

[89]https://www.amazon.com/Formule-extreme-versnelling-organisatie-Dutch/dp/9047012925

14.68 Roman Pichler

Roman Pichler is a product management expert. He has more than 15 years experience in teaching product managers and product owners, advising product leaders, and helping companies build successful product management organisations. Roman is the author of the books How to Lead in Product Management, Strategize, and Agile Product Management with Scrum. Roman writes a popular blog for product professionals, he hosts his own product management podcast, and he has created a range of product management tools.

Tip: Technical Debt And Product Success

14.69 Ron Jeffries

Ron Jeffries has been developing software longer than most people have been alive. He holds advanced degrees in mathematics and computer science, both earned before negative integers had been invented. His teams have built operating systems, compilers, relational database systems, and a large range of applications. Ron's software products have produced revenue of over half a billion dollars, and he wonders why he didn't get any of it.

Tip: Working software over ... almost everything

14.70 Samantha Laing

Tip: Arrive with your whole heart

14.71 Sander Hoogendoorn

Sander is an independent dad, speaker, writer, and traveler. He has been writing code since 1984 and still codes every day. He is a serial CTO, code philosopher, agilist, and acted as Capgemini's global agile thought leader before going freelance in 2015. Following his adagio that small steps are the fastest way forward, Sander helps to empower organizations, teams, and individuals, and to disrupt their ways of working, technology, architectures, and code. He has authored various books and published tons of articles. Sander is a well-known and inspiring keynote speaker at international conferences on diverse topics such as disruption, culture, (beyond) agile, continuous delivery, microteams, monads, software architecture, microservices, and writing beautiful code.

Tip: We are continuously uncovering

14.72 Selena Delesie

Selena helps individuals and organizations shift into freedom to create, connect, perform, and lead. She embraces conscious living from human, heart, and soul-centric lenses for lasting positive transformation. She is invited to speak and teach on Agile, Quality, Leadership, and Wellness topics. Selena can also be found growing organic food, guiding yoga, meditation, and dance circles, and exploring nature with loved ones. Join her at SelenaDelesie.com[90].

Tip: Slow Down, Then Speed Up

---

[90]http://SelenaDelesie.com

14.73 Shane Hastie

Shane Hastie joined ICAgile in 2017 as the Director of Agile Learning Programs. He has oversight in the strategic direction and expansion of ICAgile's learning programs, including maintaining and extending ICAgile's learning objectives, providing thought leadership and collaborating with industry experts, and supporting the larger ICAgile community, which includes more than 110 Member Organizations and over 95,000 ICAgile certification holders.

Over the last 30+ years Shane has been a practitioner and leader of developers, testers, trainers, project managers and business analysts, helping teams to deliver results that align with overall business objectives. He spent 15 years as a professional trainer and consultant specialising in Agile practices, business analysis, project management, requirements, testing and methodologies for SoftEd in Australia, New Zealand and around the world.

Shane was on the Board of the Agile Alliance[91] from 2011 until 2016 and is the Chair of the Agile Alliance New Zealand. He is the Lead Editor for Culture & Methods on InfoQ[92]

"I firmly believe that humanistic way of working and the agile mindset are desperately needed in organisations all around the globe today. Taking agile values and principles beyond software is important and making sure they are properly embedded is absolutely crucial for success – we're in an industry that touches every aspect of people's lives and massively influences society as a whole and I want to be a part of making sure that industry is both ethical and sustainable."

---

[91]https://www.agilealliance.org/
[92]https://InfoQ.com

Tip: Manage the shape of your backlog

14.74 Siddharta Govindaraj

Siddharta is an interdisciplinary coach. Sometimes he works with teams on how they can improve their process, at other times with leaders on organisational impediments and still other times getting hands dirty and working with individuals on better design and coding techniques. He is the author of the book Test Driven Python Programming[93]

Tip: Build your network

14.75 Stacey Ackerman

Stacey knows what it's like to be a marketer, after all she's one of the few agile coaches and trainers that got her start there. After graduating from Journalism school, she worked as a content writer, strategist, director and adjunct marketing professor.

She became passionate about agile as a better way to work in 2012 when she experimented with it for an ad agency client. Since then she has been a Scrum Master, agile coach and has helped with numerous agile transformations with teams across the globe.

Stacey speaks at several agile conferences, has more certs to her name than she can remember and loves to practice agile at home with her family.

---

[93]https://www.amazon.com/Test-Driven-Python-Development-Siddharta-Govindaraj-ebook/dp/B00VQF59D6/

As a lifelong Minnesotan, she recently relocated to North Carolina where she's busy learning how to cook grits and say "y'all".

Tip: There's no one-size-fits-all approach

14.76 Stacia Viscardi

Stacia Heimgartner Viscardi has been practicing agile and lean techniques since 2003. Over the years, she has traveled to 23 different countries to teach and coach a variety of companies to help them think about and practice better ways of working. She has been a CST with the ScrumAlliance since 2006 and recently became part of the leadership team of the Open Leadership Network. Stacia co-authored The Software Project Manager's Bridge to Agility[94] (2008) with Michele Sliger and authored The Professional ScrumMaster's Handbook[95]. Her current work in progress is Failagility: The Business of Imperfection[96]. When she is not teaching or coaching, Stacia can usually be found in a barn failing at dressage with her horse, Figo.

Tip: Letting Go

14.77 Tom Cagley

Tom Cagley is a consultant, speaker, author, coach, and agile guide who leads organizations and teams to unlock their

---

[94]https://www.amazon.com/Software-Project-Managers-Bridge-Agility/dp/0321502752

[95]https://www.amazon.com/Professional-Masters-Handbook-Expertise-Distilled/dp/1849688028

[96]https://openleadershipnetwork.com/certification/courses/failagility/

inherent greatness. His goal is to help our industry evolve through agile adoption adaptation, and measurement Tom helps teams and organizations improve cycle time, productivity, quality, morale, and customer satisfaction, and then prove it. Tom is an internationally respected blogger and podcaster for over 15 years focusing on software process and measurement. He co-authored Mastering Software Project Management: Best Practices, Tools and Techniques with Murali K. Chemuturi. Tom penned the chapter titled "Agile Estimation Using Functional Metrics" in The IFPUG Guide to IT and Software Measurement. He strives every day to help organizations recognize that change only occurs when you unlock the power of people and data.

Tip: How Act Is More Important Than What You Say You Believe

14.78 Tim Ottinger

Tim Ottinger has over 40 years of software development experience including time as an agile coach, OO trainer, contractor, in-house developer, team leader, and manager. He is also a contributing author to Clean Code, Agile in a Flash, and Clean Agile.

Tip: Curiosity Over Judgment

14.79 Tobias Anderberg

Based in the south of Sweden but working for the Stockholm based company Agical, Tobias is a Developer and Coach with over 15 years of experience in Agile. He is also a frequent speaker at conferences and co-hosts the Swedish podcast "Väg 74" focusing on software development for groups and teams.

Tip: Introverts on Agile teams, and how small changes can make a big difference

14.80 Tobias Fors

I am a consultant and educator for software developing businesses since 1999. During the years 2000-2018 I was a partner in Swedish consulting firm Citerus which pioneered the introduction of agile in Sweden. Since 2018 I work in my new company Holifant. I am a Certified Scrum Trainer since 2006. In my consulting I help clients improve without buzzwords and focus on collaborative and systemic improvement. As a trainer, I use a an experiential approach to help create valuable lasting insights.

Tip: Zoom Out

14.81 Tom Perry

Tom Perry is a transformation consultant and coach, a frequent writer, speaker and author on Agile topics, and founder of the Agile Management Northwest conference.

Tip: Going Viral

14.82 Tony Ponton

Tony Ponton has been an IT Professional for over 20 years and an Agile-Lean Practitioner, Coach and Trainer since 2002.

He specialises in coaching leaders, individuals and organisations in agility in order to build high performing organisations.

He co-chairs one of the world's leading Agile Podcasts – The Agile Revolution[97] and is part of the global Heart of Agile[98] movement and serves as a Heart of Agile Method Guide.

Tony believes in harnessing and enabling the power of human interaction and their unique and innate ability to respond dynamically and creatively to any problem or situation.

Agility at it's heart provides the guiding imperatives to achieve this.

I am driven by helping organisations, people and teams to understand how to use agility to thrive, improve and amplify their natural potential.

Tip: Creating Collaborative Connective tissues

14.83 Terry Harmer

Originally hailing from Ireland, Terry Harmer has spent the past number of years as a Scrum Master, Agile Coach and Chapter Lead guiding teams, leaders and organizations on their Agile journeys.

Terry considers himself a pragmatic Agilist and draws from a wide variety of approaches and experiences to help people (not resources![99]) to discover better ways of working.

A proponent of the power that comes from unlocking the unique skills and insights that each individual brings and

---

[97]https://theagilerevolution.com/
[98]https://heartofagile.com/
[99]https://www.hanoulle.be/2011/05/19/human-resources/

wary of one size fits all solutions. Terry believes Drucker said it best when he stated that "Culture eats strategy for breakfast"

You can follow Terrys Agile journey on instagram @agileterry[100]

Tip: Stop, Collaborare And Listen

14.84 Tsutomu Yasui

Tsutomu (☒) Yasui (☒☒), as known as Yattom, is a freelance agile coach living in Tokyo, Japan.
He started his agile journey in early 2000 with Extreme Programming which he still loves.
He has been fond of games since his childhood which eventually lead him to create his own card games and board games.
Psychological Safety Game is best known among others, like Agile Treasure Hunt Game or The Kanban Game.
He likes to work together with teams, sometimes programming by himself, and plays those games to deepen the understanding of agile, combined with retrospectives.
He lives with his wife Akiko and two Shiba-Inu dogs, Kinako and Kurumi.

Tip: Mind the short and the long

14.85 Tze Chin Tang

Tze Chin TANG is an experienced Agile practitioner, coach and trainer with over 15 years in modern software product and team development. His experience includes building high

---

[100]https://www.instagram.com/agileterry/

performing teams and organisations via adoption of Agile methods, practices and other modern ways of working. As part of his professional Agile Coaching practice, Tze cultivates environments of connectedness and collaboration, crucial to enable high performing teams. Tze is the founder of Futurework.Asia, an Agile Coaching, Consulting and Training practice, which explores, provide education and advises on adopting ways of work. His clients included e-Commerce, financial services, broadcast solutions, cloud products and market expansion services. He has led agile transformations where he was responsible for designing structure, governance, and operational environment to optimise performance in teams to deliver fantastic results to their customers.

Tip: It's not just the question you ask, but how you ask it!

14.86 Vasco Duarte

I want to transform product development organizations into product business organizations. I do that by focusing the work of the product development teams on the end-to-end lifecycle of their products. From Concept to Cash and Back!
Product Manager, Scrum Master, Project Manager, Director, Agile Coach are only some of the roles that I've taken in software development organizations.
I host a daily podcast where I interview Scrum Masters about their daily challenges and insights[101]
You can join me on twitter: @duarte_vasco[102]

Tip: Two simple heuristics that will solve (most of) the problems you face as a Scrum Master

---

[101]https://scrum-master-toolbox.org/
[102]https://twitter.com/@duarte_vasco

14.87 Woody Zuill

Woody Zuill is an Agile and Lean Software Development guide and coach. He has been programming computers for almost 40 years and is an originator and pioneer of the Mob Programming approach to teamwork in software development. He provides workshops and training on team software development. He is also a founder of the "No Estimates" discussion, and a frequent speaker at conferences and user group meetups.

Tip: Turn Up the Good

14.88 Yassal Sundman

Yassal Sundman is a team coach consultant and teacher working at Crisp[103] living in Stockholm. She enjoys the day to day work of interacting with people and helping them discover better ways of working.Fix It Now or Delete it[104] is her side project helping teams manage bugs by not managing them! You can follow her blog[105] or reach her at yassal.sundman@crisp.se

Tip: Coaching By Listening

14.89 Yves Hanoulle

Yves Hanoulle (he/him) discovered extreme programming in 1999. Over the years, he realised that creating working soft-

---

[103]http://www.crisp.se
[104]http://www.FixItNowOrDeleteIt.com
[105]http://blog.crisp.se/author/yassalsundman

ware takes collaborating over writing code. Just like coaching is asking questions over sharing ideas.

Yves is an independent consultant, a Creative Collaboration Agent with more than 15 years of experience, working around the globe. Yves has been helping small and large companies as a FireStarter and an agile instigator.

The agile community knows Yves from his many contributions including the public agile conferences Google calendar[106], his Agile Thursday Quiz, the coach retreats[107], daily coaching questions via @Retroflections[108], and the Agile Games Google group[109]. Since 2004 he has been promoting PairCoaching, an idea which has been adopted by many agile trainers and coaches.

Yves is constantly learning and passing on what he learns as a coach and trainer to organisations large and small. He gives free lifetime support[110] on anything he does: every client, everything he writes and presents, every workshop he leads.

Yves believes in maintaining a sustainable pace both professionally and personally. He's a big fan of WorkLifeFusion. He has done talks and workshops with his father, partner and also his three kids. When Yves is working from home, he is working on his walking desk[111].

Yves has parentpair programmed an android game with his 13 year old son[112] You can learn more about Yves[113], and find

---

[106]http://agileconferenc.es

[107]http://coachretreat.org

[108]http://retroflection.org/

[109]https://groups.google.com/g/agilegames

[110]https://www.hanoulle.be/2011/09/22/fls-free-lifetime-support/

[111]https://www.hanoulle.be/2013/02/16/im-working-from-a-walking-desk/

[112]http://www.anguis.be

[113]http://www.hanoulle.be/yves-hanoulle/

him on social media as @YvesHanoulle[114].

Tip: Study the manifesto

14.90 Zuzi Zuzana Sochova

Zuzana "Zuzi" Šochová is an independent Agile coach and trainer and a Certified Scrum Trainer with the Scrum Alliance with more than 15 years' experience. She has implemented Agile transformation and implementation in many companies and teams around the world. By creating and sustaining Agile leadership, she believes the worlds of work and life can be happier and more successful. She is the founder of the Czech Agile Association and the AgilePrague conference, a member of the Scrum Alliance board of directors, and an author of The Great Scrum Master: #ScrumMasterWay. She can be reached at zuzi@sochova.com or via Twitter @zuzuzka.

Tip: Collaboration

---

[114]https://twitter.com/yveshanoulle

15. Resources

- Mike Beedle Support page[1]
- Norm Kerth Support page[2]
- Jean Tabaka fund[3]

- The new new product development game[4], Hirotaka Takeuch & Ikujiro Nonaka
- The Scrumguide[5], Jef Sutherland & Ken Schwaber
- The Scrum Alliance[6]
- The Scrummaster toolbox[7], Vasco Duarte
- Mountain Goat Software[8], Mike Cohn
- a-reusable-scrum-presentation[9]
- Product Owner in a nutshel video[10], Henrik Kniberg
- Retroflection[11] Archive of 7 years of daily twitter questions.
- Agile conferences Calendar[12] all agile conferences worldwide, maintained by a community of +400 people.
- xebia essentials cards[13]

---

[1]https://www.gofundme.com/mikebeedlesupport
[2]http://www.processimpact.com/norm_kerth.html
[3]http://Www.fund4jean.com
[4]https://hbr.org/1986/01/the-new-new-product-development-game
[5]https://www.scrumguides.org/
[6]https://scrumalliance.org/
[7]https://scrum-master-toolbox.org/
[8]http://www.mountaingoatsoftware.com
[9]https://www.mountaingoatsoftware.com/agile/scrum/resources/a-reusable-scrum-presentation
[10]https://www.youtube.com/watch?v=502ILHjX9EE
[11]http://retroflection.org/
[12]http://agileconferenc.es/
[13]http://essentials.xebia.com/

- MyDailyThankYou[14] twitter tag invented by Chris Matts[15]
- Kudo cards online[16]
- A3 Thinker for iOS: 65 Brainstorming Cards for Lean Problem-Solvers[17]
- Speed of trust action cards[18]
- Groeten uit Delft: great vlog with tips from agile community leaders [19]
- Library of Trust[20]
- Agile Fluency Model[21]
- The Core Protocols[22]
- Mob Programming for the Introverted[23]
- A webcomic of romance, sarcasm, math and language[24]

---

[14]https://twitter.com/search?q=%23mydailythankyou
[15]https://twitter.com/PapaChrisMatts
[16]http://kudobox.co/
[17]https://a3thinker.com/ios/
[18]https://www.amazon.com/Speed-Trust-Action-Cards/dp/B00KD0KPY8/
[19]https://www.youtube.com/channel/UC940VJCgGX2eZzpGxbirUeQ
[20]http://www.hanoulle.be/2015/03/the-library-of-trust/
[21]http://www.jamesshore.com/Blog/Agile-Fluency-Model-Updated.html
[22]https://liveingreatness.com/core-protocols/
[23]https://www.agilealliance.org/resources/experience-reports/mob-programming-for-the-introverted/
[24]https://xkcd.com/

16. Library

- The Scrummguide[1], Jef Sutherland & Ken Schwaber
- Agile Retrospectives[2], Esther Derby & Diana Larsen
- Extreme Programming Embrace Change [3], Kent Beck
- Extreme Programming Embrace Change Second edition[4], Kent Beck & Cynthia Andres
- Crystal Clear[5], Alistair Cockburn
- Large Scale Scrum [6], Craig Larman & Bas Vodde
- Dynamics of Software Development [7], Jim McCarthy
- Leading Geeks[8], Paul Glen
- X-teams[9], Deborah Ancona & Henrik Bresman
- Leading teams[10], Richard Hackman
- Training From the back of the room[11], Bowman

[1]https://www.scrumguides.org/

[2]https://www.amazon.com/Agile-Retrospectives-Making-Pragmatic-Programmers-ebook/dp/B00B03SRJW

[3]https://www.amazon.com/Extreme-Programming-Explained-Embrace-Change-ebook/dp/B00N1ZN6C0/

[4]https://www.amazon.com/Extreme-Programming-Explained-Embrace-Change-ebook/dp/B00N1ZN6C0/

[5]https://www.amazon.com/Crystal-Clear-Human-Powered-Methodology-Small/dp/0201699478

[6]https://www.amazon.com/Large-Scale-Scrum-More-Addison-Wesley-Signature-ebook/dp/B01JP91OR4

[7]https://www.amazon.com/Dynamics-Software-Development-Jim-McCarthy/dp/1556158238/

[8]https://www.amazon.com/Leading-Geeks-Manage-Deliver-Technology-ebook/dp/B000VI1XLQ

[9]https://www.amazon.com/X-teams-Build-Teams-Innovate-Succeed/dp/1591396921

[10]https://www.amazon.com/X-teams-Build-Teams-Innovate-Succeed/dp/1591396921

[11]https://www.amazon.com/Training-Back-Room-Aside-Learn/dp/0787996629

- The Pragmatic programmer[12], Andrew Hunt & David Thomas
- Management 3.0[13], Jurgen Appelo
- Succeeding with agile[14], Mike Cohn
- Scrum and XP from the trenches[15], Henrik Kniberg
- Toolbox for the agile coach[16], Jimmy Janlén
- The Responsibility Proces[17], Christopher Avery
- User Story Mapping[18], Jeff Patton
- Agile software development with scrum[19], Ken Schwaber & Mike Beedle
- Coaching agile teams[20], Lyssa Adkins
- Scrum mastery[21], Geoff Watts
- Working Effectively with legacy code[22], Michael Feathers
- The great Scrummaster[23], Zuzana Sochova
- Scrumban[24], Corey Ladas

---

[12]https://www.amazon.com/Pragmatic-Programmer-Journeyman-Master/dp/020161622X

[13]https://www.amazon.com/Management-3-0-Developers-Developing-Addison-Wesley/dp/0321712471

[14]https://www.amazon.com/Succeeding-Agile-Software-Development-Using/dp/0321579364/

[15]https://www.infoq.com/minibooks/scrum-xp-from-the-trenches-2

[16]https://leanpub.com/agiletoolbox-visualizationexamples

[17]https://www.amazon.com/Responsibility-Process-Unlocking-Natural-Ability-ebook/dp/B01LYB6QV1/

[18]https://www.amazon.com/User-Story-Mapping-Discover-Product-ebook/dp/B00NF07FHS

[19]https://www.amazon.com/Agile-Software-Development-Scrum/dp/0130676349

[20]https://www.amazon.com/Coaching-Agile-Teams-ScrumMasters-Addison-Wesley-ebook/dp/B003QP47YG

[21]https://www.amazon.com/Scrum-Mastery-Geoff-Watts-ebook/dp/B00D6WWN7C/

[22]https://www.amazon.com/gp/product/B005OYHF0A

[23]https://www.amazon.com/Great-ScrumMaster-ScrumMasterWay-Addison-Wesley-Signature/dp/013465711X/

[24]https://www.amazon.com/Scrumban-Essays-Systems-Software-Development-ebook/dp/B004SY63BY/

- The software projects manager's Bridge to agility[25], Michele Sliger, Stacia Broderick Viscardi
- An Agile Adoption and Transformation Survival Guide[26], Michael Sahota
- Specification by example[27], Gojko Adzic
- The phoenix Project[28], Gene Kim, Kevin Behr, George Spalford
- The age of agile[29], Steve Denning
- The Leader's Guide to Radical Management: Reinventing the Workplace for the 21st Century[30], Steve Denning
- Reinventing Organisations[31], Frederic Laloux
- Open Minds[32], Andy Law
- The Psychology of Computer Programming[33], Jerry Weinberg
- Becoming a Technical Leader[34], Jerry Weinberg
- Fearless Change: Patterns for Introducing New Ideas[35], Linda Rising
- Thinking Fast and Slow[36], Daniel Kahneman

[25]https://www.amazon.com/Software-Project-Managers-Agility-Development-ebook/dp/B004YW6M5C/

[26]https://www.infoq.com/minibooks/agile-adoption-transformation

[27]https://www.amazon.com/Specification-Example-Successful-Deliver-Software/dp/1617290084

[28]https://www.amazon.com/Phoenix-Project-DevOps-Helping-Business-ebook/dp/B078Y98RG8/

[29]https://www.amazon.com/Age-Agile-Smart-Companies-Transforming-ebook/dp/B072J5XPTP/

[30]https://www.amazon.com/Leaders-Guide-Radical-Management-Reinventing-ebook/dp/B0043M4ZPW

[31]https://www.amazon.com/Reinventing-Organizations-Creating-Inspired-Consciousness-ebook/dp/B00ICS9VI4/

[32]https://www.amazon.com/Open-Minds-Andy-Law/dp/1587990466

[33]https://www.amazon.com/Psychology-Computer-Programming-Silver-Anniversary/dp/0932633420/

[34]https://leanpub.com/becomingatechnicalleader

[35]https://www.amazon.com/Fearless-Change-Patterns-Introducing-Ideas-ebook/dp/B0054RGYNQ/

[36]https://www.amazon.com/Thinking-Fast-Slow-Daniel-Kahneman-ebook/dp/B00555X8OA/

- First break all the rules[37], Marcus Buckingham, Jim Harter
- Joy inc: how we built a workplace people love[38], Richard Sheridan
- Company-wide Agility with Beyond Budgeting, Open Space & Sociocracy[39], Jutta Eckstein
- The Anatomy of Peace[40], The Arbinger Institute
- Systemantics (The Systems Bible)[41], John Gall
- Scrum Field Guide[42], Mitch Lacey
- Collaboration Explained[43], Jean Tabaka
- Essential Scrum[44], Kenneth S Rubin
- Nonviolent communication[45], Marshall B Rosenberg
- Five dysfunctions of a team[46], Patrick Lencioni
- Never Split the Difference[47], Chris Voss
- 96 visualisation examples[48], Jimmy Janlén
- Radical Candor: Be a Kick-Ass Boss Without Losing Your Humanity[49], Kim Scott

---

[37]https://www.amazon.com/First-Break-All-Rules-Differently-ebook/dp/B01E7M6INO/

[38]https://www.amazon.com/Joy-Inc-Built-Workplace-People-ebook/dp/B00DMCW1FK

[39]https://leanpub.com/bossanova

[40]https://www.amazon.com/Anatomy-Peace-Resolving-Heart-Conflict-ebook/dp/B00SGET4BS/

[41]https://www.amazon.com/SYSTEMANTICS-SYSTEMS-BIBLE-John-Gall-ebook/dp/B00AK1BIDM

[42]https://www.amazon.com/Scrum-Field-Guide-Addison-Wesley-Signature-ebook/dp/B019PFBM3O/

[43]https://www.amazon.com/Collaboration-Explained-Facilitation-Software-Development-ebook/dp/B001U5VJWC/

[44]https://www.amazon.com/Essential-Scrum-Practical-Addison-Wesley-Signature-ebook/dp/B008NAKA5O/

[45]https://www.amazon.com/Nonviolent-Communication-Language-Life-Changing-Relationships-ebook/dp/B07C6JQZ7H

[46]https://www.amazon.com/Five-Dysfunctions-Team-Leadership-Lencioni-ebook/dp/B006960LQW

[47]https://www.amazon.com/Never-Split-Difference-Negotiating-Depended-ebook/dp/B014DUR7L2

[48]https://www.amazon.com/Visualization-Examples-Jimmy-Janl%C3%A9n/dp/9188063011/

[49]https://www.amazon.com/Radical-Candor-Kim-Scott/dp/B01KTIEFEE

- The Culture Code: The Secrets of Highly Successful Groups[50], Daniel Coyle
- Evolutionary Anatomy of Test Automation Code[51], George Dinwiddie
- Patterns of Agile Journeys[52], George Dinwiddie, Susan DiFabio, Oluf Nissen, Rich Valde, Dan Neumann
- Quiet:the power of introverts in a world that can't stop talking New York[53], Cain, Susan. (2012)
- Four meanings of introversion: Social, Thinking, Anxious, and Inhibited Introversion.[54], Jonathan Cheek, et al
- The seven habits of effective people[55]
- Accelerate[56] by Nicole Forsgren[57], Jez Humble[58] & Gene Kim[59]
- Drive[60], Daniel Pink[61]
- The Goal[62], Eli Goldratt[63]
- The fearless organisation[64], Amy Edmondson[65]

---

[50]https://www.amazon.com/Culture-Code-Secrets-Highly-Successful-ebook/dp/B01MSY1Y6Z

[51]https://leanpub.com/EvolutionaryAnatomy

[52]https://leanpub.com/agilejourneys

[53]https://www.amazon.com/Quiet-Power-Introverts-World-Talking-ebook/dp/B0074YVW1G/

[54]https://www.academia.edu/7353616/Four_Meanings_of_Introversion_Social_Thinking_Anxious_and_Inhibited_Introversion

[55]https://www.amazon.com/Habits-Highly-Effective-People-Powerful-ebook/dp/B00GOZV3TM

[56]https://www.amazon.com/Accelerate-Software-Performing-Technology-Organizations-ebook/dp/B07B9F83WM

[57]https://twitter.com/nicolefv/

[58]https://twitter.com/jezhumble

[59]https://twitter.com/RealGeneKim

[60]https://www.amazon.com/Drive-Surprising-Truth-About-Motivates/dp/1594484805

[61]https://twitter.com/DanielPink

[62]https://www.amazon.com/Goal-Process-Ongoing-Improvement-Anniversary/dp/B00IFGGDA2

[63]https://www.amazon.com/Eliyahu-M-Goldratt/e/B000APWH4C

[64]https://www.amazon.com/Fearless-Organization-Psychological-Workplace-Innovation/dp/1119477247

[65]https://twitter.com/AmyCEdmondson

- From Contempt to Curiosity: Creating the Conditions for Groups to Collaborate Using Clean Language and Systemic Modelling[66], Caitlin Walker[67]
- The Listening Space[68], Tamsin Hartley[69]
- Better Allies[70], Karen Catlin[71]
- Good Guys[72],David G Smith, Brad Johnson
- Blindspot (hidden biases of good people)[73], Mahzarin R Banaji[74]

---

[66]https://www.amazon.com/Contempt-Curiosity-Conditions-Collaborate-Modelling/dp/B00LI6YHGS/
[67]https://twitter.com/caitlinwalkerTA
[68]https://www.thelisteningspace.co.uk/the-book
[69]https://twitter.com/listeningspace2
[70]https://www.amazon.de/-/en/Sally-McGraw/dp/1732723354/
[71]https://twitter.com/kecatlin
[72]https://www.amazon.de/-/en/David-G-Smith/dp/1633698726
[73]https://www.amazon.de/-/en/Mahzarin-R-Banaji/dp/0345528433/
[74]https://www.amazon.de/-/en/Mahzarin-R-Banaji/e/B00DVPMT9Q/

17. Versions

17.1 The e-book

The e-book version can be found at LeanPub.
https://leanpub.com/TipsFromTheTrenches[1]
It was first released on 2018/06/26

17.2 The audio book addition

In 2019 Yves collaborated with Vasco Duarte to create an audio addition to the book.
This audio addition can be bought on the Oikosofy website.

The https://oikosofyseries.com/tips_from_the_trenches_the_-audio_project[2]

This version was first released on 2019/12/09

17.3 The paper version

The paper version of the book can be bought on all amazon sites.

https://www.amazon.com/Yves-Hanoulle/e/B07RNGH3LJ[3]

It was first released on 2021/10/25

---

[1]https://leanpub.com/TipsFromTheTrenches
[2]https://oikosofyseries.com/tips_from_the_trenches_the_audio_project
[3]https://www.amazon.com/Yves-Hanoulle/e/B07RNGH3LJ

18. Errata

Errata of the book after this publication can be found here[1]

(If you bough the E-book on leanpub, you can always download the latest version.)

---

[1]https://www.hanoulle.be/book/tips-from-the-agile-trenches/

Printed by Amazon Italia Logistica S.r.l.
Torrazza Piemonte (TO), Italy

26030403R00172